THIN AIR

THIN AIR

The Life and Mysterious Disappearance of Helen Brach

By
Pat Colander

Contemporary Books, Inc.
Chicago

Library of Congress Cataloging in Publication Data

Colander, Pat.
   Thin air.

   1. Brach, Helen Marie Vorhees.   2. Missing
persons—United States—Biography.   I. Title.
HV6762.U5B73   1982   364.1'5 [B]   82-45437
ISBN 0-8092-5801-3

Copyright © 1982 by Pat Colander
All rights reserved
Published by Contemporary Books, Inc.
180 North Michigan Avenue, Chicago, Illinois 60601
Manufactured in the United States of America
Library of Congress Catalog Card Number: 82-45437
International Standard Book Number: 0-8092-5801-3

Published simultaneously in Canada by
Beaverbooks, Ltd.
150 Lesmill Road
Don Mills, Ontario M3B 2T5
Canada

For Paul

Contents

Acknowledgments   ix

Part I: The Disappearance

1 The Last Weekend of Helen Brach   3
2 The Story of Helen Vorhees of Hopedale, Ohio   13
3 Mr. Matlick and Mrs. Brach   21
4 Frank V. Brach and His Wives   28
5 Helen Vorhees and Frank Brach
  Live Happily Ever After   37
6 Mrs. Brach and the Animals   42

Part II: The Investigation

7 Helen Brach Is Missing   51
8 Continental Bank vs. Helen Brach   58
9 The Investigation as Conducted by the Officers
  of the Chancery Division of the Circuit Court
  of Cook County   70
10 The Last of the Litigation   81

Part III: What Happened
11 The Morris Ferguson Connection   93
12 Charles Vorhees Tries Again   100
13 The Horse Traders and Silas Jayne   103
14 Helen Brach and the Horse Traders   113
15 Jack Matlick and the Perfect Crime   117
16 The End of the Cold Trail   121
17 A Final Resting Place   126

Acknowledgments

Thanks to the wonderful people who made this book possible: Jeanette Ansell, Debora Christopher, Mary Connors, John Drummond, Bob Enstad, Tom Greer, Fred Kravitz, Mike Lenehan, Tom McCarthy, John Cadwalader Menk, Lee Morrison, Bonnie Taman Owens, Charles Peterson, Ernie Rizzo, Mary Ryan, and Dr. Marv Rosner.

And special thanks to little Charlie, who helped out in his own sweet way.

THIN AIR

"An Angel Visited the Earth One Day
and Took a Beloved Flower Away."

> Inscription carved on the gravestone
> of Helen Brach's mother.

PART I
THE DISAPPEARANCE

1

The Last Weekend of Helen Brach

It was about half past ten in the morning on Thursday, February 17, 1977, when Helen Brach, the sixty-five-year-old widow of one of the three founders of the Chicago-based E. J. Brach & Sons candy company, Frank Brach, and heiress to a fortune in property and securities estimated at that time to be worth $21 million, placed what was probably the last phone call of her life from her room at the Kahler Hotel in Rochester, Minnesota, where many Mayo Clinic outpatients stay.

She called Jack Matlick, the fifty-two-year-old caretaker of the eighteen-room house set on seven acres just off Wagner Road in Glenview, a suburb north of Chicago, which had been her main residence for the last thirty years. Telephone company records obtained by the police department of the Village of Glenview showed that she had been in constant contact with Jack Matlick during her four-day stay in Minnesota, making numerous short calls home. However, they talked for about forty-five minutes during her last morning in Rochester.

She may have been discussing the subject of her second-to-last phone call, which she had made approximately one-half hour earlier to Douglas Stevens, a former Brach company executive and a friend of both Mrs. Brach and her late husband. Stevens lived with his wife Adalene in Ft. Lauderdale, Florida. The Stevenses normally met her at the airport when she flew down for a visit, and she had called to tell them that she would not be arriving in Florida on Monday, February 21, as she had originally intended. Helen Brach had made appointments for that last week in February with a Ft. Lauderdale beautician and with an attorney who was finalizing her purchase of a $200,000 condominium in the Sunrise East development—a complex of buildings overlooking the South New River Canal, the intracoastal waterway that passes through town—and the appointments would have to be changed. She would be arriving soon, she advised the Stevens. She just was not exactly sure of the date yet.

There is some speculation, however, that she and Jack Matlick may have been discussing the pending termination of Matlick's eighteen years of service to the Brach family, or at least a major change in his status. And there is every reason to believe that the change was coming because Mrs. Brach was thinking of moving permanently away from the Chicago area.

That winter, which was far from over, had been one of the cruelest ever. By early November 1976 the first blasts of cold air had rolled off Lake Michigan and the temperature had dropped below freezing a half dozen times in Chicago. A few weeks passed before the storms hit, along with the high winds and the blinding snow. January had been even more brutal. Drafts were everywhere that drafts were unusual. A young couple stranded in their car on Interstate 57, just south of the city, were found frozen to death. Blizzards raged across the Midwest. Frank Brach had died during a similar cold wave seven years earlier in January 1970.

If the miserable winter weather was not reason enough to move away, there was also the fact that Helen Brach had no friends in Chicago. She shunned the role of society matron and rich dowager. The few people who saw her on a regular basis—Jack Matlick and his wife, an elderly woman who came from the far southeast side of the city to clean her house, the neighbor whose kitchen window faced her door, several tellers at the Glenview State Bank who cashed small personal checks for her—were not likely to notice the chic, mature woman who looked young for her age, who stood about five feet, ten inches, weighed about 160 pounds, and most often wore her long, heavy red hair braided and pinned up at the back of her head. She tinted her hair now that she was getting older, and sometimes she would fool those who did recognize her with a dark brunette or platinum wig. Only her brown eyes were unmistakable. Her eyes and her cars, that is. Helen Brach owned five cars, and each was very distinctive: a dark lavender Rolls Royce convertible, a pink Cadillac convertible, a salmon-colored Cadillac sedan, a fire engine red Cadillac convertible, and a pearl pink Lincoln Continental.

The only local person outside of the Brach household for whom Helen Brach seemed to hold any affection was a North Shore playboy and horse trader named Richard Bailey. Bailey was a compact fellow and a snappy dresser, and he was seventeen years younger than Helen Brach. He lived in an apartment on Lake Shore Drive in Chicago, and he owned the Bailey's Stables on Harms Road in the suburb of Morton Grove, adjacent to Glenview. According to what Richard Bailey told the Glenview police, he first met Mrs. Brach at a car wash in 1975, and they had been fast friends ever since. Jack Matlick, however, said that Mrs. Brach had been dating Bailey a couple of years before that. Though it was impossible to ascertain the nature of the relationship between Mrs. Brach and Mr. Bailey by the winter of 1977, Bailey himself said that he was in New York with Helen Brach on New Year's Eve of 1976, attending Guy Lombardo's annual party at the Waldorf-Astoria.

After Helen Brach met Richard Bailey she became involved in a series of horse deals, often with Bailey's older brother Paul, known as P. J. All together she purchased at least nine horses for a total of about $200,000. One of the horses, for which she paid $50,000, turned out to have a bone disease, making it practically worthless. And there is a persistent rumor that Helen Brach gave Richard Bailey as much as $100,000 for a horse shopping trip to Argentina, a trip that never produced a horse.

Whatever the nature of her tie to Richard Bailey, it was probably not strong enough to keep her in Glenview. She once said that she could never marry anyone who did not have as much money as she did, and Richard Bailey, whose annual income the police have estimated was in the hundreds of thousands of dollars, was not even in Mrs. Brach's league.

Perhaps the best evidence of Helen Brach's desire to abandon the Chicago area entirely was the increasing amount of time during the summer that she spent at the large ranch house that Frank Brach had built for her late father, Walter Vorhees, some twenty years earlier at Tappan Lake, Ohio. A resort community, Tappan Lake is about a twenty-minute drive from the town of Hopedale, where Mrs. Brach was born.

There were a few people she was close to in southeastern Ohio. There was Maybelle Thomas, matronly in appearance, grey-haired, and slightly overweight—the antithesis of the glamorous Helen Brach—who lived next door to Walter Vorhees in another house Helen and Frank built and who took care of the old man until he died. Carol Ledfors was a willowy blonde, a younger woman by some twenty-five years, who was shy and soft-spoken most of the time, and who, like Mrs. Brach, was devoted to animal causes and pet welfare. The two women became friends when a scandal erupted at the Harrison County, Ohio, dog pound in 1974 when it was found that the local dogcatcher was selling the stray mutts he picked up to a laboratory, which used the animals for scientific experiments.

Charles Vorhees, Helen Brach's younger brother, was all that was left of her family, and the two were quite friendly despite the fact that some said Charles's wife did not care much for her wealthy sister-in-law. A quiet man with a distinguished appearance, Charles Vorhees was recently retired from his job inspecting railroad cars for Conrail. He lived comfortably on his pension, atop a ridge at the edge of Hopedale in a sprawling house with a built-in swimming pool that was a gift from his sister.

But the most striking symbol of Helen Brach's strong connection to the region where she grew up was the imposing monument to the Brach and Vorhees families she had built at the cemetery in Unionport, Ohio, about ten miles away from Tappan Lake. Walter and Daisy Vorhees were buried there, as was Frank Brach and two of Helen's favorite dogs, Candy and Sugar. For herself, she had prepared a tomb with a bower of roses sculpted in granite and marble and her name carved in curving script.

The question of whether Helen Brach's relocation in Ft. Lauderdale was to be a temporary or permanent arrangement was not certain. But it was certain that just prior to that intended trip to Florida in 1977 she went to the Mayo Clinic in Rochester, Minnesota, for a checkup. Her ankles, she noticed, had swollen recently and she was vaguely afraid that she might be getting arthritis. Generally, even the most rich and powerful cannot get into the Mayo Clinic without making an appointment months in advance. Helen Brach was able to forgo the wait, however, because her friend Richard Bailey knew somebody at the hospital. Bailey had used his influence on at least one other occasion to get a well-to-do, unattached, older woman from the Chicago area of Rogers Park an appointment when he had escorted a Mrs. Karstenson to and from Rochester, Minnesota, the year before. He managed to get Helen Brach admitted for Valentine's Day.

Soon after Helen Brach finished her telephone conversation with Jack Matlick she took her Samsonite suitcase and purse and left her room at the Kahler. She stopped at the desk and paid her bill with a personal check, number 4921, written on an account at the Glenview State Bank. Then Mrs. Brach returned to the Mayo Clinic across the street from the hotel, leaving her bag with a clerk there. At the clinic she received a final medical report, which showed negative results from a battery of tests and pronounced her to be remarkably healthy. One of the doctors lectured her about getting some exercise and losing a little weight. With check number 4922 she paid her bill at the hospital.

Even when Chicago was having a mild winter, there were extreme cold spells in Rochester, which is 150 miles farther north. For that reason there is an arcade running underneath the street that separates the Mayo Clinic from the Kahler Hotel. After Mrs. Brach left the clinic around one o'clock she took the tunnel back to the hotel. En route she stopped at one of the specialty stores, a bath shop in the tunnel, and charged on her American Express card a set of towels and a matching alabaster-colored soap dish and powder box, a $41 purchase. She instructed the salesclerk, Phyliss Redalen, to mail the merchandise to her new home in Florida. Everett Moore, the Chicago accountant who had handled the Brach's money for more than twenty-five years, would receive the bill at his office on Wacker Drive near the banking district on the southwest end of the Chicago Loop.

Mrs. Redalen, an elderly woman, chatted with Mrs. Brach, who looked striking that day, wearing a full-length mink coat with her red hair braided and pinned up. Mrs. Brach had seemed to be in quite a hurry but nevertheless took the time to fret when choosing the color for the bathroom accessories she was purchasing. Helen Brach was in a good mood, the saleslady thought. She told Mrs. Redalen that she had just received a clean bill of health from the clinic and that she had recently purchased a Florida condominium and was excited at the prospect of furnishing the new place.

Months later, when the clerk was interviewed by a private investigator, she said that Mrs. Brach had said that her "houseman" was waiting for her. Mrs. Redalen was sure that Helen Brach had said "houseman," rather than "horseman," she told the police, to clear up any possible confusion. In other words, Mrs. Brach had probably been making reference to Jack Matlick rather than Richard Bailey. The saleslady was not sure, however, if Mrs. Brach meant that the houseman was waiting for her outside the shop, somewhere in Rochester, at O'Hare Airport, in Glenview, or in Florida.

Helen Brach left the arcade shop, presumably stopped back at the hotel, and went from the Kahler to the airport, where she was supposed to catch Northwest Airline's flight 352, which would arrive at O'Hare Airport about 3:00 P.M. Chicago time. A local cab driver would recall for a detective that he had taken a woman who fit Helen Brach's description to the Rochester Municipal Airport that afternoon, and Northwest Airline would verify the fact that Helen Brach's ticket had been used that day. However, none of the members of the flight crew would be able to remember that they had seen her on the plane when the police asked them about it.

On Thursday afternoon, according to phone company records, Jack Matlick—or an unknown person—called a number of airlines from the Glenview residence and had a series of brief one- and two-minute conversations. Then Matlick, who said he was the only person home that afternoon, went out to run a few errands before he was scheduled to meet Helen Brach, whom he referred to as "Mrs. B" or "the Missus," at O'Hare. Though his employer owned a small fleet of luxury automobiles, Jack Matlick told the police that he was driving a four-wheel-drive jeep when he met Mrs. Brach. He said that his boss was a little upset about having to ride home in such a vehicle, but he had explained to her that he had run short of time and was unable to switch cars. As it was, he was late in fetching her. According to Matlick, he and Helen Brach left the airport terminal area about 4:00 P.M. and rode back to the Glenview house, a trip that normally would take about an hour.

By 5:30 that evening someone was back at the estate because a phone call went out from Glenview to a farm in the northwest suburb of Schaumburg, where Jack Matlick lived with his wife and daughters. The farm, which had been part of the Brach real estate fortune since the Depression, was provided for the houseman's family rent free, one of the fringe benefits of Jack Matlick's job. Authorities presumed that

Matlick called his wife that evening, when, according to his version of the story, he and Mrs. Brach returned from the airport.

Jack Matlick may have had a good reason to call home. Authorities later theorized he may have informed his wife that this was to be an unusual weekend. Helen Brach had a longstanding policy: when she was in town, Matlick lived in Schaumburg and worked an eight-hour shift in Glenview. When she was out of town, he lived at the Brach house. Jack Matlick would swear to the police that Helen Brach was home this particular weekend, but he remained in Glenview anyway. He had some extra work to do around the house and grounds, he said.

Over the next few days there was a rash of phone calls to and from the household. Nothing was out of the ordinary about that. It would have been strange if the phone had been quiet, for Helen Brach used the telephone compulsively. Also, one of the horses she had purchased through Richard Bailey had won a race at the track at Hialeah, Florida, just south of Ft. Lauderdale, and friends were phoning their congratulations. However, none of those well-wishers, when queried, said that they actually spoke with Helen Brach.

Only one of the weekend callers, an older woman who occasionally worked for Mrs. Brach as a maid, told police that she had spoken with the mistress of the house. However, the authorities concluded later that she was sometimes confused and had probably been mistaken.

Glenview Police Chief William Bartlett, a soft-spoken greyhaired man with a wizened face, who was going to retire in a few years, found it unusual that Mrs. Brach was supposedly at home, yet had spoken to no one. "Mrs. Brach, we learned, was a person who ordinarily used the phone extensively. Yet an examination of the list of calls that were made from her home during that time, and interviews with people who tried to phone her on those days, have established that she apparently had personal contact with no one."

Richard Bailey called from Florida late Sunday night, February 20, and Jack Matlick answered the phone. The houseman said he was surprised to hear from Bailey because he had presumed that Mrs. Brach had gone out on a date with him. Somebody, he was no longer sure who, had picked Mrs. Brach up that afternoon, Matlick told Bailey. Later, Matlick told the police that Helen Brach had returned home around midnight. The rest of the callers that weekend either received no answer or were told by Matlick that Mrs. Brach had just stepped out, was in the bathtub, was indisposed, or was just unable to come to the phone at the moment.

Of the calls that went out from the house, there were five to various Marshall Field department stores. On the last call a meat grinder attachment for the blender had been ordered by a man later identified as Jack Matlick.

There was a call to Frank Brach's one-time physician—a man Helen Brach had not seen since her late husband's funeral seven years before. The call was answered by the doctor's service. It is not known who placed the call, but the doctor later told police that he had no idea why Mrs. Brach would have tried to call him. Jack Matlick offered no explanation. The accountant Everett Moore also was called from the Glenview house. The call was picked up by Moore's answering machine, but the caller left no message. Police believed Helen Brach knew that Everett Moore was never in his office over the weekend. On Sunday evening Jack Matlick phoned a cleaning and decorating service to make an appointment for a crew to come as soon as possible to repaint two rooms and replace a rug. The service agreed to send people out on Tuesday.

Matlick said that on Sunday, February 20, he watched his employer sign a number of checks that totaled $15,000, $12,400 of which went to him. The checks, numbered 4924 and 4925 and 4976 though 4981, were typewritten and dated February 17 and 18. These checks paid Jack Matlick $1,000 for his monthly salary and provided another $3,000 he said was a post-season Christmas bonus. The houseman also claimed that he was given $2,944.29 to pay the balance on an auto loan he had taken to finance his new jeep and $5,500 that was going to Matlick to allegedly buy back a Cadillac once owned by the

Brach family, given to Matlick, and sold by Matlick in 1976. There was a check for $1,000.40, a reimbursement of money Matlick said he had spent running the house, and $1,000 was designated as a deposit for a piece of equipment Matlick was to buy for use at the Schaumburg farm where he lived. Jack Matlick also cashed a check for $700 that he said Mrs. Brach took as pocket money for the Florida trip.

The gifts were an incredible display of generosity on the part of Helen Brach. Her employees were used to getting Christmas presents of less than $50. Even her donations to animal welfare organizations were rather measly as compared to those made by other wealthy donors. She had two or three favorites—one was the Animal Protective Institute of Sacramento, California—that received contributions in the $10,000-$20,000 range. But a handful of others received gifts of $100 or less.

The signature on those checks looked different, Matlick said, because Mrs. Brach's right wrist had been injured when a trunk lid fell on it while she was packing for the trip to Florida.

It was another freezing Monday morning when he took Mrs. Brach back to O'Hare Airport at about 7:00 A.M., said Matlick. Almost three hours before the earliest scheduled flight to Florida, Jack Matlick drove Mrs. Brach to the airport in the salmon-colored Cadillac with its HVB license plate. Though she often traveled with as many as forty pieces of luggage, this time, according to Matlick, Helen Brach carried only a small tan overnight bag. She did not even take the trunk with which she had hurt her hand while packing. Instead she told Jack Matlick that she would call him in ten days with instructions about sending all the other clothing she had packed. The last time Jack Matlick alleged he saw her, she was wearing a black suit, a white blouse with a black bow tie, and matching black patent leather shoes and purse. In the description Jack Matlick originally gave the police there was no mention of any kind of a coat or her wounded and bandaged hand.

2

The Story of Helen Vorhees of Hopedale, Ohio

IT was not very surprising that nobody missed Helen Brach at first. She kept her distance from other people. In fact, she rarely went out of the house on Wagner Road. One of her employees said that she infinitely preferred good carryout chicken to a fancy downtown dinner.

Her nearest neighbors characterized her as vain and reclusive. The children who rushed her house on Halloween were greeted by the gruff, dark-haired, five-foot-ten figure of Matlick, who dispensed not Brach candy, but modest amounts of Butterfingers, a Curtiss candy bar, or Hershey chocolate. Helen Brach had no patience with kids, her neighbors told reporters.

She kept up with a few girlfriends she knew from Hopedale High School in Ohio, and a couple of them claimed that they were very intimate, but, when the police questioned them they did not seem to know her as well as they said they did.

Of her acquaintances in and around Chicago, only the handyman Matlick said he was privy to all her secrets. He told people that she confided in him that she disliked sex and was not physically capable of intercourse because her vaginal opening was not large enough. When Frank Brach's will was probated in 1970 his widow had been asked several pointed questions about the character of her friendship with Matlick. Her answers were not on record.

Neighbors described Jack Matlick as brusque and very protective of his employer. Matlick could be very intimidating. John L. Demand, Jr., a one-time Glenview police detective, talked with Robert Enstad of the *Chicago Tribune* in a 1979 interview and defined the Brach-Matlick partnership this way: "For lack of a better word I'd call it Brachism. They had this aura of money and importance about them, and they believed they had this little kingdom. Mrs. Brach seemed to look upon herself as queen. He [Matlick] thought he was the queen's general manager."

If Jack Matlick was telling the truth, it would seem they had a special relationship. Yet the impression Mrs. Brach gave was that their "friendship," if it could be called that, was less than satisfactory. At least one associate felt that Helen Brach thought that the people who really loved her—her husband and her parents—were all dead.

Everett Moore, the money manager, was supposedly friendly with Helen Brach. It was alleged by Charles Vorhees that Moore was in Ft. Lauderdale, stayed at Mrs. Brach's apartment, and drove one of her cars just prior to her disappearance. But the accountant was a quiet, elusive old gentleman whose relationship with Helen Brach had always been somewhat mysterious. Few people had seen or spoken with him. Mr. Moore emerged only once publicly, years after Mrs. Brach disappeared, and that was to give a court deposition. He testified that Mrs. Brach had spoken to him about her personal unhappiness after suffering a series of misfortunes. "She had repeated to me . . . a feeling that she was perhaps, say, unlucky. First she lost her mother, and then she lost her father, and then she lost her husband . . . in a period of six years, and she felt very close to her parents. So there was some remorse there. . . ."

In autumn 1977, when Helen Brach's disappearance had

been public knowledge for six months, a distant cousin, Susie Sullivan, who worked as a sales representative in the western suburbs, summarized the situation: "I feel so sorry for her. No one seems to care."

Helen Brach's standoffishness may have had its roots in her ethnic and regional background. In many ways she exhibited the traits common to the people she grew up with in Ohio.

Today coal mining is the dominant industry in the hilly Appalachian country Helen Brach came from, though about 10 percent of the land is still given over to farming. A typical county has about eight or ten towns of various size and importance, and each contains about 10,000–15,000 people. They are German, Norwegian, Irish, and Italian, and they do not have much money. This generally depressed area was staunchly Republican until the middle 1950s, when the coal mines were in full operation and the voters became union members and Democrats. Mining is on the wane now, business is bad, and according to Charles Peterson, editor of the *Harrison News-Herald,* many of the residents voted Republican in the last election. "The area is expected to come back," Peterson said. But in the meantime, he explained, it is not a bad place to live. "The people are friendly and open and willing to help. The fact that it is a rural area means that it's safe." The Harrison County area is cleaner than the Ohio Valley and naturally beautiful—there are three lakes in the district. The people of Jefferson and Harrison counties (Helen Brach lived in both at one time or another) are proud of their communities.

The Vorhees family seems to have been typical of the people of this area. Born of German-Irish stock, these families have been as staid as they were long-lived. On one hand, they are pleased with their heritage and the ability to trace their roots back several centuries. The local libraries are full of histories with stories of Ohio families carefully compiled over the years by the residents and printed at their own expense. But at the same time, these people are extremely private and loyal to members of their clan. They solve their own problems. They hide their black sheep and do their own dirty laundry. They cling together and live in the same sections for many, many years.

Helen Brach was one of the few members of her family to leave southeastern Ohio, and she may have proved the axiom about it being better to stick close to home. Some of her small-town neighbors cannot help but feel that once outside Hopedale and Unionport she was swallowed up by the forces of evil.

Her ancestry made her proud, and she frequently used the name Helen Vorhees Brach. She saw to it that her parents' gravestones were engraved not only with their full names and birth dates, but also with those of their parents.

The Vorheeses were originally part of a group of German settlers who came to America in about 1670. There were two Jacob Voorheeses—a father and a son—who left New Jersey and eventually got to Ohio some time before 1803. The elder Jacob was a slight man. He weighed about 130 pounds, in striking contrast, his neighbors suggested, with the rest of the men in the family who were all big, hearty fellows.

Jacob was a tailor who might have remained in New Jersey for his whole life, were it not for his son's adventuresome ways. The younger Jacob first traveled to Wellsburg, West Virginia, where he learned to be a cabinetmaker. Wellsburg was then at the edge of the frontier, the Far West. Some time around 1800 the young man pushed on farther to Jefferson County, Ohio, where he built a log cabin on a piece of wild land. He then sent for his father and the rest of the family, and they were soon established.

Several years went by before Jacob struck out on his own again. This time he traveled back East a bit to Fayette County, Pennsylvania, where he made cabinets and met Elizabeth Gaskell, the daughter of a soldier in the Revolutionary War. Elizabeth and Jacob were married, and a few years later they returned to Jefferson County.

Jacob Voorhees had done well making closets in Pennsylvania, and in March 1833 he purchased 172½ acres of uncleared land in North Township in Harrison County. Jacob and Elizabeth's eldest child, Samuel Sickles Voorhees, was four years old then, and North Township was barely settled. By most accounts there were no white settlers in this part of Ohio until 1796 or 1797. About 1805—the time Jacob built his first cabin—the pioneers began sectioning off parts of the land in counties and townships and, during the next couple of decades, local governments sprang up. Typically, southeastern Ohio townships were built on high, rolling land. There were a few steep and rough spots, but grains and grasses found firm support in the limestone soil. Underneath that soil was a layer of coal, but the early settlers were farmers and sheepherders and showed no interest in the fuel until more than 100 years later. By the mid-1800s these townships might have contained a couple of villages, two or three railroad stations, a handful of post offices, a dozen churches, and at least one main road. Samuel Voorhees settled in one of these little villages, where he was the miller.

Samuel had seven brothers and a sister, and they had all been fruitful and multiplied. Only the sister had moved away from the area. As the family grew the spelling of the name changed to Vorhes and Voorhes and finally Vorhees, but they were the same group. Jacob the elder was their common father and great-great-grandfather to Helen Brach.

By 1880 Samuel Vorhes's family was living in the town of Unionport. Unionport then had a population of 300 and was located at Cross Creek on the Pennsylvania Railroad. The town was not very old, having been first laid out in 1859, and Samuel Vorhes was one of Unionport's first postmasters and treasurers.

The Vorhes family had branched out in terms of interests— there were Vorhes who were doctors—but they had not expanded much in terms of location. Most of the family members stayed in the area, married other local folk, and had children who stayed in the area and married more local folk.

On April 30, 1863, Samuel and Amanda had a son, Anson, who was reared in the Jefferson County schools and later took up his father's occupation. He learned both the carpentry and millwright trades, but he built his reputation in the latter field. Anson worked for eighteen years as a miller and was called for consultation to different parts of the country. The history books say that "no man in Jefferson County . . . had more real experience in this difficult line of work."

Anson and Ada Vorhees had three children, who by the year 1910 were all working at the post office. The oldest, Walter, born May 18, 1886, was a mail carrier for the rural free delivery out of Unionport, Mae was the assistant postmaster there, and Lulu, the youngest, worked as a clerk. Anson had pledged the Vorhees family to the Republicans, was a member of the Unionport lodge of the Knights of Pythias, and was a man who "exerts considerable influence in this section," according to an early biographical record.

On July 8, 1911, Walter Vorhees appeared in the Jefferson County Probate Court before Judge J. R. McCeland, swore that he was twenty-five years old, a Unionport resident, and a streetcar driver, who wanted to marry Daisy Rowland. Daisy vowed that she had also been born in Unionport and had never been married before. She gave no occupation, and she lied about her age. She was really twenty-seven, but Daisy Rowland swore that she was also twenty-five. Judge McCeland noted for the record that a Reverend Rowland was expected to solemnize the ceremony later.

Walter and Daisy's first child, a daughter, was born four months and three days after that, on November 11, 1911. They called the baby Helen Marie. It was about seven years before her little brother Charles was born.

Even before Helen Vorhees was beautiful, she was striking— a gangly youngster with bean-pole legs and carrot-colored hair. She filled out when she was a teenager, and by the time she graduated from Hopedale High School she was one of the most attractive girls in the class. Shortly after high school she married a local boy, following small-town custom. That marriage did not last long. Helen Vorhees grew tired of her husband's frequent indiscretions. By the time she was twenty-one years old they were divorced. Eventually the county records of that marriage disappeared, but Helen Vorhees never forgot about it. Thirty years after the divorce she told a girlfriend that she might have been able to make that marriage work if she had only been sexier.

Her first job was selling tickets for the Toronto-Steubenville Interurban, a local transportation company. Then she went to work at the Scio Pottery Factory in Scio, Ohio. The Depression had made it difficult for the tableware manufacturer—the only industry for miles around—but it had survived and provided jobs for about 1,000 people who came from within a radius of twenty-five miles from towns like Urichsville, Midvale, Amsterdam, Hopedale, and Apple Creek.

Helen Vorhees was twenty-nine years old when she got a job at the factory in April 1941. Lena Hiller, a petite woman with light brown hair, is semiretired now and works at the pottery office a few days a week. Then she was secretary to the plant's owner, Lou Reese. Helen Vorhees came to work from Unionport, ten miles away, over a twisting country road. Though she started out as a cup finisher, she was soon promoted to the office, where she worked alongside Lena Hiller as a billing clerk. Lena Hiller said the most memorable thing about her were her looks; she was a very attractive woman. "She had such beautiful hair. It was a red-gold, and she always wore it in a long braid wound around the top of her head." She was still wearing it that way the last time Mrs. Hiller saw her in about 1975, when Helen went back to Scio for a street fair in the summertime. Even after Helen left Unionport, was married, and went to Chicago, she kept up with her friends in Ohio, Mrs. Hiller said.

In December 1943 she quit the pottery factory to take a job selling dance tickets at the Starlight Ballroom at Buckeye Lake. The resort community about thirty-five miles from Columbus, Ohio, hosted name entertainers and big bands and drew a fancy crowd from Cleveland. Though Helen Vorhees remained in touch with her family and few friends in Unionport, she was intrigued with this new lifestyle. While she was working at the Starlight, she heard about a job opening at a club in Florida.

There is a photographic portrait of Helen Vorhees that was made in the late 1940s. (The picture first appeared publicly in a magazine in 1978.) Helen Vorhees was about twenty-five years old and quite stunning, a Susan Hayward–type redhead. It was not difficult to imagine Frank Brach noticing her when they met a few years later in 1950. Helen Vorhees was working as either a hostess or a hatcheck girl (depending on who is telling the story) at the posh Indian Creek Country Club in Miami Beach. One night Frank Brach was there with his second wife. The couple had a raucous public argument in the lobby of the club and then left together. Later that night Frank Brach returned alone and asked Helen if she would like to join him for a drink. Helen Vorhees seldom dated, but she accepted Frank Brach's invitation.

3

Mr. Matlick and Mrs. Brach

THE house where Helen Brach lived in Glenview is at its most scenic and splendid during the dead of winter. Set back from the main road by a wide, grassy slope covered with snow, the stately home is surrounded by fir trees that set off the white wooden trim without barricading the windows. A circular drive curves toward the main entrance where four wooden columns support a gabled canopy. Eight shuttered windows line the second floor, and were they not offset by the pointed roof, the house might have looked like a barracks. Downstairs, there are two bay windows and two large terrace doors that emit so much light that one might get the feeling of living in a glass house. At the south side of the drive there is a great brick box of a garage with its own attic and steeple. The picture that is created is framed on either side by a forest of large leafless maple and elm trees. When traffic is light the place seems particularly serene.

For two weeks following Helen Brach's alleged departure

for Ft. Lauderdale, Jack Matlick spent most of his time alone at the mansion. After he dropped Mrs. Brach at the airport, he said, he went home and gathered some of her jewelry and then took it to deposit in a lock box at the Glenview State Bank. The bank opened at 9:00 A.M., and Matlick was there by 9:05. After he left the bank he drove the salmon-colored car to a Park Ridge Cadillac agency and had the upholstery shampooed and the exterior waxed. On Tuesday the decorators came. When police questioned the workers who had done the car and house jobs they learned there had been nothing unusual about the original condition.

Belton Mouras, the chief executive of the Animal Protective Institute, who had become a close associate of Helen Brach, spoke frequently to his organization's number one benefactor. Mouras had found her in good spirits when he talked to her the weekend of February 12. During that conversation Mouras promised to call her again when she returned to Glenview from the Mayo Clinic the following weekend. But, when Mouras tried her number on Sunday, February 20, he received no answer. Mouras tried again late in the evening, about an hour before Richard Bailey called and spoke to Jack Matlick, but still he received no answer. Three or four days after that Mouras called again. This time Jack Matlick answered the phone.

Jack Matlick told Belton Mouras that Mrs. Brach had gone to Ft. Lauderdale. When Mouras inquired where she had been the previous Sunday when he tried to reach her, Matlick allegedly told him she "was out with Rich Bailey that night."

During the second week of Mrs. Brach's absence, Matlick hired a cook-housekeeper, a woman who had allegedly worked for the Brachs years before.

Each day the caretaker fed and exercised Mrs. Brach's three dogs: Luvey, Tinkerbelle, and Beauty.

Glenview Police Sergeant Joe Baumann, a hefty middle-aged cop with thick dark hair streaked with grey, first met the houseman on March 4, 1977, when Matlick went to the suburban police headquarters, a huge windowless fortress set back from Waukegan Road. Baumann and Police Chief William Bartlett were in their offices that morning, downstairs from the reception area. Jack Matlick entered the cavelike suite and spoke to both of them at the same time. He explained that he worked for Helen Brach and said that he was afraid that she had not made it to Florida—he had had no communication from her in two weeks—and he wished to file a missing-person report. Baumann told him that it was not that simple. A missing-person report could be filed and accepted only from the next of kin. Matlick returned to the estate. That afternoon he notified Charles Vorhees, who arrived from Hopedale five days later.

But before Charles Vorhees went to the Glenview police station he and Jack Matlick took it upon themselves to remove some old diaries and "automatic writings"—notes Mrs. Brach had made while in a psychic trance—that had been left in a dresser drawer in Helen Brach's bedroom.

During the last years of her life, Helen Brach would rise before the sun was up and, with a pencil hung loosely in her hand, wait for the spirit world to answer her questions by guiding her hand along a piece of paper. "Automatic writing," as the procedure is called, is almost always used to attempt communication with the dead. Though psychic experts do not consider automatic writing to be one of the higher mental methods of communication, it is by no means scoffed at. The Ouija board and direct voice statements by a temporarily possessed medium are given the same amount of respect as automatic writing as far as the experts are concerned.

The fact that Helen Brach was engaging in this type of experiment suggested that she had no suicidal tendencies. She may have known that to be an instrument of transmission she had to be in good mental and physical condition. In her book, *A Treatise on White Magic,* Alice Bailey, one of the foremost authorities on psychic phenomena, says that would-be mediums must avoid everyday traumas and emotional distractions. They have to stay away from the pitfalls of depression. To this end, Bailey says, psychics should try to maintain a certain amount of levelheadedness, good sense, mental and physical discipline, and willingness to work for the good of humankind. When these aspects are present a person is fit to be used as a transmitter or an instrument.

Though neither of them has ever adequately explained why, Jack Matlick and Charles Vorhees burned the material they found in Mrs. Brach's bedroom in the furnace of the Glenview home. Vorhees said that the manuscripts were full of information "Helen wouldn't have wanted other people reading." He claimed that he had found a note on top of the diaries written in green ink in his sister's handwriting, which said, "Burn these in case something happens to me."

Vorhees was unclear about what he thought had happened to Helen at that point and why he thought it was necessary to destroy the writings at that time. He told the police he burned the note, too. He reported to the Glenview authorities that he had not read any of the material. It was not known whether Jack Matlick had read any of the writings.

The Glenview Police investigation into the disappearance of Helen Brach commenced. As Chief Bartlett said, "It's a baffling situation. If she were abducted, there would be some contact for money. And what other motive is there?"

Police Sergeant Baumann found out that, a few months before her disappearance, Helen Brach had called a Miami, Florida, woman who "read cards" for her almost daily during that period. Those calls stopped coming on February 16.

The forged checks came to light very soon after the investigation was officially under way. Everett Moore told the police that he had stopped by the Glenview house to ask about Mrs. Brach's mail. Moore opened a bank statement he picked up from a pile that Matlick was saving for her. Moore took a good look at the eleven checks with the peculiar signatures, so unlike the tight delicate script that Moore knew well.

"Why, Mrs. Brach didn't sign these," Moore said and then repeated, "This isn't Mrs. Brach's signature."

"Well, I told you before," Matlick replied, "while she was putting some bedspreads away in a trunk, the night she got back from Rochester, the trunk lid fell on her hand and hurt it." (This was a slightly different version of Matlick's earlier explanation of Mrs. Brach's injured wrist.)

Moore went to the Glenview police and reported that he had a series of personal drafts he believed were phony. A graphologist from Continental Bank and another graphologist from the Northern Illinois Crime Lab confirmed Moore's suspicions that the checks were forgeries. Crude forgeries. The signatures did not resemble Mrs. Brach's signature in the least. The last legitimate check authored by Helen Brach was for her transportation to and from Rochester, Minnesota. It had been written days before the bogus ones.

The discovery of the checks raised more questions than it answered. Everett Moore told the police that Jack Matlick had never received a Christmas bonus that large and that his petty cash expenses rarely exceeded $400. Jack Matlick did not have much to offer in the way of explanation. He said that Helen Brach had probably given him the money to pay off his jeep and buy back the old Cadillac because she was "sentimental."

Also, the appearance of the forgeries posed the first of many legal dilemmas that arose from Mrs. Brach's status as a missing person. Although the bank or the police could swear out a complaint against whomever they thought had done the forgery, prosecution would be difficult without Mrs. Brach present to act as a witness. There were too many unanswered questions precluding legal action.

None of the airlines were able to produce any evidence to back up Jack Matlick's story that Helen Brach had taken a plane to Florida. The earliest flight scheduled the Monday morning when he said she left had been set to go at 9:50 A.M. The police could not find anyone at O'Hare Airport who remembered the ostentatious pastel car. Conceivably, Helen Brach could have slipped on board an airplane using an assumed name, the police supposed. But why would she do such a thing? And, even if she had decided to "become invisible," she would have needed a large amount of cash to pull off a charade of such magnitude. Helen Brach carried very little cash as a matter of course and there was only Jack Matlick's word that she had taken $700 with her.

Charles Vorhees and Jack Matlick gave the Glenview police permission to search the estate. But when the police combed the house and grounds they found few things that interested them. They came across a newspaper clipping about urban crime lying on top of a pile in a desk tray. The article, dated February 2, was headlined, "Will We Always Live in Fear?"

A pile of ashes and metal binders that would not burn were left in the furnace. The earth around the house was frozen, as it had been for at least forty-two days, making it very difficult to bury any evidence. Over the next few weeks the police made several searches of the house, which proved equally fruitless. On one of those searches they noticed that the newspaper article was gone from the desk tray.

Jack Matlick was extremely cooperative with Bartlett and Baumann. But Helen Brach's behavior during the last weekend he had seen her, as reported by Matlick himself, just did not make sense to anyone who knew her habits, and Matlick had to be considered a suspect in the event of a possible crime. In his own defense, Matlick told the police that he was not named in Mrs. Brach's will.

There is a discrepancy in the story of *how* Matlick knew he was not named in the will. Matlick maintained that during the first weekend of the investigation he had given the police a copy of Mrs. Brach's will, which he said he had found in the house. The police claimed that Matlick never brought them any such document.

Sergeant Baumann told Matlick to get a lawyer. The handyman's handwriting was analyzed, and it was determined by the same experts who had discovered the forgeries that Matlick had not forged the checks.

The police did not seem very interested in finding out who had written the phony checks, however. Matlick's wife, for instance, was not tested. As far as anyone knew, Matlick's wife had not even been questioned by the police. Though it was never explained, the police somehow came to the conclusion that the forgeries were the work of more than one person.

Matlick was forthright about his friendship with Mrs. Brach. One night, when the police visited him at the Brach house, he suddenly broke off their conversation and adjourned to another room. He returned with a small metal container, flipped it open, and showed them a strand of red hair. Matlick said that the hair belonged to Helen Brach, and he stroked it as he talked. One of the police officers present said that the handyman became increasingly agitated as he talked about Mrs. Brach. "The way his buttocks moved back and forth," the policeman said later, "I thought he was going to come."

It was after one of these impromptu visits by the police that Matlick had special locks installed on three doors at the Glenview house: Mrs. Brach's bedroom, her study, and her closet. The new maid said that when she needed to go inside any of the three rooms Matlick would open the door and stand and wait until she was through. Jack Matlick was simply protecting his employer's property, he told police.

At the Cook County Sheriff's Office, Chief of Police Edmund Dobbs offered the county facilities when the houseman volunteered to take a lie detector test. The Glenview police decided, for the record, that the results were inconclusive. However, Jack Matlick's attorney supposedly conceded to a newspaper reporter that the police told his client that he had flunked not one, but two, polygraph tests.

Matlick himself felt that he was being convicted by the press, but it had not affected his job status. His wife and children stayed on at the Schaumburg farm, and Jack Matlick continued to live in Helen Brach's house, tend to the animals, and collect his paycheck from Everett Moore, just as though nothing strange or unusual was happening.

4

Frank V. Brach and His Wives

HELEN Vorhees had done well to catch Frank Brach's eye. Not only was he a millionaire many times over; he was also still a handsome man—long, lean, and tan, his hair gone white at the temples. He was almost sixty and did not have to devote as much time to the candy business as he had had to when he was younger. He arranged rendezvous with Helen in Florida and in Pittsburgh, the closest big city to Unionport, Ohio.

Their romance was complicated by Frank Brach's wife.

Frank Brach married his second wife, June, in Miami Beach, Florida, in February 1933. The couple had been together seventeen years, had no children, and, for the last few years, lived in the large house on Wagner Road in Glenview.

According to June Brach their marriage started to dissolve with the first terrible quarrel in 1945, and that session left her with a bruise where Frank had hit her. Then there was another occasion when Frank came to blows with her in August 1948. June moved out on May, 5, 1949, after Frank demanded that she leave. She was afraid that her husband was capable of "using personal violence" against her, she said in her divorce complaint against him, so she had to vacate the home and move to separate quarters at 5510 Sheridan Road in Chicago—an older, brick apartment building on the lake—while Frank remained at the Glenview estate.

Apparently some attempt at reconciliation was made, because the two vacationed in Miami together in 1950. They quarreled in Florida, where Frank met Helen Vorhees. But the final indignity as far as June Brach was concerned was a fight at the Glenview house on January 16, in which Frank pushed her against a stone wall and hit her. She said that her husband acted without provocation, that he was very angry with her, and that the struggle left a bruise on her shoulder.

June Brach's accusations were almost identical to the charges made by the original Mrs. Brach in the first divorce case twenty years before. June was well aware of the large settlement Frank had paid after that proceeding, and she intended to do her level best to get what she considered her due.

There were some similarities in the two lawsuits, and there were some differences.

Frank Vincent Brach was about to turn twenty-five when he was married to Eunice Essig in January 1915. The next year the couple had a son, Frank V. Brach, Jr., and a year after that the Brach Candy Co., which was flourishing, was incorporated. Their daughter Joyce did not appear until nine years later, at about the same time they moved into a mansion at 175 Sheridan Road in Winnetka, just down the road from Frank's brother, Ed.

In the summer of 1930 Frank and Eunice had a disagreement that Eunice said ended with Frank physically abusing her. The marriage went sour after that incident, and when the matter went to court the next year it was Eunice who explained what had happened. In her divorce petition Eunice Brach told the court that she had lived and cohabited with Frank for fifteen years and "at all times treated her husband with kindness and forbearance, and conducted herself toward him as a chaste, dutiful and affectionate wife, bearing with her husband's faults and errors and striving to make their home comfortable and happy." Frank, Eunice said, had not been so easy to get along with. In spite of what he had said in his marriage vows, he had been "guilty of extreme and repeated cruelty. . . . [T]hat frequently . . . he struck, beat, slapped and otherwise ill-treated and abused her . . ." that during the month of December, 1929, at their home in Winnetka, "[Frank] struck [Eunice,] bruising her and causing her to suffer great pain; that again in August of 1930, at Woodruff, Wisconsin, [Frank] struck [Eunice,] . . . that again in December of 1930, at their home in Winnetka, [Frank] struck [Eunice]. . . ."

The following summer Frank left their North Shore home and told his wife that he was not coming back. That was when she filed for divorce. Frank Brach countered Eunice's charges in his answer to her petition. Basically, his attorneys wrote that Eunice had not been a very good wife. (Frank's petition implied that she had not lived up to her wifely duties as they were outlined in the marriage ceremony.) But, Frank added, he had never grown impatient enough to physically abuse her.

On September 14, 1931, Eunice Brach went before Cook County Circuit Court Judge Otto Kerner to make her statement in person. (Judge Kerner was the father of another Otto Kerner, who would become famous as the only Appeals Court Justice to be found guilty of high crimes.)

When Mrs. Brach's attorney asked her what Frank's treatment of her had been during the time they were married she said that Frank had had a terrible temper. She went on to explain that they had many arguments over the years and that they had a particularly bad argument at Christmastime almost two years earlier. "He became enraged because I didn't get a party for New Year's Eve at the South Shore Country Club to his liking. He just pushed me all around the room." Eunice Brach's lawyer, Sidney Gorham, asked her if Frank had struck her, and Eunice said that he had. Then he inquired about the quarrel the year before in August, in Woodruff, Wisconsin. "Well," Eunice replied. "He didn't want to go down to my mother's and father's for supper, so I told him I promised to go and intended to go. So he wouldn't let me have the car and chauffeur, so I called a Yellow cab, and he came out to the cab after me and pulled me out and made my arm black and blue." Gorham then asked for the specifics of what had happened in December 1930. Mrs. Brach explained that there had been many incidents similar to that one when "he would fly into a rage and strike me." The lawyer asked if Mrs. Brach had agreed on a settlement with her husband, and Eunice said that she had.

Judge Kerner interrupted. He wanted to establish what the current situation was with the family. Eunice Brach told him that she had not been living with Frank Brach as his wife since November 1, 1930, and reiterated that the property settlement he had offered was fine with her.

"I will state for the benefit of the court and for the record that Mr. Brach is creating a trust fund of $1,000,000 in bonds, the income from which is to be paid to Mrs. Brach during her lifetime," Sidney Gorham said. "Under the agreement she is to have the right to occupy the residence in Winnetka during her lifetime, or until she abandons it, and have use of the household furniture. He is paying her in money or securities $50,000, and according to the terms of the trust instruments, after Mrs. Brach's death the income will go to her children, unless the trust is revoked." Gorham asked Eunice Brach again if she understood the terms. Judge Kerner asked her if everything had been explained thoroughly to her. Sidney Gorham added that under the terms of the settlement, Joyce and Frank, Jr., would remain with their mother ten months out of the year. During that time Eunice was responsible for their support and education. Their father had the right to see them at all reasonable hours and to have them visit him not more than two months each year.

Even though Eunice sounded anxious to end the ordeal and was extremely amicable about the agreement, the laws at that time made it necessary for the courtroom scenario to continue a while longer. After Eunice stepped down, her sister, Helen Holm, took the stand and testified that Frank Brach had a "very violent temper." She had seen him drag Eunice out of a taxicab, and occurrence that left her sister scratched and "bruised her arm pretty badly." Frank Brach was in the habit of going into rages, she added, and she never knew when it might happen next. Alfred Holm, Helen's husband, swore that he, too, had seen the taxicab argument and that he had seen Frank Brach hit his wife on more than one occasion. "When he loses his temper, he uses his arms and fists," Alfred said. When he finished his testimony, Gorham told Judge Kerner that he had another witness and Kerner replied that it would not be necessary. The judge asked Andrew Ryan, Frank Brach's attorney, if he wanted to do any cross-examination and if he and his client understood everything. The agreement was fine as far as the defense was concerned, Ryan said, and Kerner told Gorham to prepare the necessary documents. The divorce decree was signed the next day. Eunice Essig Brach and her two children got a million-dollar trust fund, and Frank Brach got out of the fifteen-year marriage.

Frank Brach could easily afford to set up such a large trust fund. By 1930 the Brach family had become very wealthy, and they operated the candy empire from a factory at 4656 W. Kinzie Street, near the western border of Chicago. E. J. Brach & Sons employed more than 2,000 people and manufactured 400 varieties of candy, about 100 million pounds each year. The Kinzie Street plant was a model for its time, built to make distribution easy. On one side of the building were loading docks for the trucks. Brach's owned 150 trucks that were refrigerated in hot weather and could haul up to 10,000 pounds of candy each. Candy that was being shipped farther than 750 miles away was loaded out of the back door of the factory onto freight cars.

Brach's had a huge, modern laboratory, equipped for testing raw materials and developing new production methods. There were five graduates of the Massachusetts Institute of Technology among the eleven engineers employed by Brach. The Brachs had come a long way from their storefront sweet shop.

The candy business was booming in Chicago in the 1930s, and Brach's was doing better than any other company. All together there were 200 varieties of confections coming out of the Midwest, and a quarter of those recipes belonged to E. J. Brach & Sons.

The complex operation of the 1930s was the idea of Frank Brach's father, Emil, who was born in Schoenwald, Germany, in 1867. Emil was seven years old when he came to the United States. He lived and attended school in Burlington, Iowa, then a semithriving metropolis along the Mississippi River. Burlington, in the southern part of Iowa, was within striking distance of Ft. Madison and Keokuk, which also had large German immigrant populations. Like so many others of that generation, Emil J. Brach left the farm and made his way to the big city. The young man arrived in Chicago in 1880, almost a decade after the Great Fire had wiped out most of the major companies. The candy industry, which had been going fairly strong there for forty years, was in the process of rebuilding. The new factories had steam equipment for cooking. A few even had installed packaging machines to wrap the sweets. Emil Brach learned the trade and worked his way up. From 1896 until 1904, E. J. Brach was president of the Dreibusheim Company, a confectionery firm. He left Dreibusheim to start his own candy business with the help of his two teenage sons.

The current television advertising campaign for Brach's calls it "the old-fashioned candy store candy." In the beginning that was exactly what it was. Emil Brach opened a store called the Palace of Sweets on North Avenue in 1905. At first, Edwin, who was sixteen, and Frank, age fourteen, were all the staff necessary for the little store. Keeping the records and cutting and packing the candy were Edwin's jobs. Frank was the salesman. Emil Brach was the inventor and innovator, a pioneer soon to become a legend in the candy-making trade.

Emil Brach may have been doing things the old-fashioned way, but he had no intention of keeping tradition. He disdained hand methods for making candy. Those techniques were expensive and time-consuming. A tinker by nature, he developed utensils and simple machines and implemented them as he went along. Under his auspices, candy making became an engineering project. One of the first major breakthroughs was the development of a method of conveying a gas flame to the bottom of a tilting candy kettle without interruption. His next idea was to make a machine for dipping taffy-on-a-stick, an improvement that cost $1,000, the total assets of the Brach company at the time.

Nor could E. J. Brach leave the recipes alone. The elder Brach played with the mixtures the same way he played with machines, adding and subtracting ingredients just as he added and subtracted mechanical parts. Particularly fond of caramels, he tried baking them instead of stir-cooking them. The Brach pan caramel revolutionized the candy business. Brach caramels were easier and more efficient to make. They were also more appealing because they were less sticky and they could be sold at half the price of other caramels.

What Emil Brach did for candy making, his son Frank did for candy marketing. During the 1920s Frank Brach had a brilliant idea for retailing candy. He sold a thousand pounds of pan caramels to Siegel, Cooper, & Co., a Chicago department store. Overnight the Brachs were the leading wholesale candy manufacturers. That caramel sale assured Frank Brach's fortune.

In 1950, June Brach's lawyers were hard at work trying to estimate exactly how big that fortune was. Emil Brach had been dead for three years by then and Edwin was president of the company. Frank was vice-president.

When June Brach filed for separate maintenance at the end of May 1950, she also served notice on the Continental Bank, First National Bank of Chicago, Northern Trust, Harris Bank, and the National Safe Deposit Company—everywhere she knew Frank had accounts or safe deposit boxes. She was afraid that Frank would make good on his threat to cut her off financially and was trying to make sure that he would be unable to hide his substantial assets. June complained ". . . that all during married life . . . Frank V. Brach has given his love, attention, care, and consideration to his two children by a former marriage to the exclusion of June; that he preferred the company and attention of his . . . children on vacations rather than the company of June; that he informed June on a great number of occasions that she should get out and leave the domicile. . . . [T]hat on a number of occasions he has used personal violence toward June, leaving marks and bruises on her arms and body, which together with Frank V. Brach's conduct and treatment . . . has rendered her life miserable."

In her petition June went on to say that she had income, but it was not sufficent to maintain her "in a manner commensurate with her way of life." She was no longer able "to pay all her expenses, clothe herself, entertain and travel on her . . . income in the same manner she formerly lived." June placed Frank Brach's net worth at between $5 million and $6 million and said that he had threatened to dispose of all his assets rather than support her. She wanted the court to freeze Frank's accounts and order him to pay her $400 a week.

Frank denied every word of June's complaint and said he was not worth a penny more than $3 million. June's attorney's came back with an amended complaint for divorce. This time they cited three specific occasions when Frank Brach had physically abused her.

The divorce had gotten to be quite a mess. June learned that Frank had been meeting Helen Vorhees in hotel rooms. She hired a lawyer in Steubenville, Ohio, and on October 27, 1950, a summons was issued to Helen Vorhees of Unionport. June sued Helen for alienation of affections; she wanted $100,000 in damages.

June Brach's strategy and persistence paid off. Seeing no way out of the situation, Frank Brach decided to bargain.

By the time the whole sordid affair came to trial on November 13, 1950, a deal had been made that would give

June Brach $100,000 in cash and $300,000 to be paid in $20,000 increments over a period of fifteen years regardless of whether or not she remarried. June Brach's niece, Darlene McCartney, and her husband, James, testified that day that they had visited the Brachs often at their home and had seen the results of the couple's vicious quarreling and Frank's angry tirades. Both told the court that they had seen June very upset and bruised as a result of unprovoked attacks by her husband.

The divorce decree, signed November 17, legally assured June's award, found that Frank Brach was guilty of extreme and repeated cruelty, and stated flatly that both Frank and June were worth more money than either of them had been willing to admit.

Three days later June asked the Jefferson County court to dismiss her suit against Helen "with prejudice." June Brach wanted it on record that she still had a grievance with Helen Vorhees, but she dropped the lawsuit and paid the court costs of $11.75.

When it was all over, Frank Brach went to Unionport to ask Walter Vorhees for his daughter's hand in marriage. Frank Brach and Helen Vorhees were married in 1951. Frank was sixty-one years old. His bride was thirty-nine.

5

Helen Vorhees and Frank Brach Live Happily Ever After

HELEN and Frank Brach appeared to have a happy marriage, though it was impossible to say for sure. Nobody except Jack Matlick was close enough to tell, and Jack Matlick was not talking. Also, Frank Brach had a tendency to stay in marriages he did not like. His two failed marriages had lasted fifteen years and seventeen years, respectively.

The third Mrs. Brach moved into the opening left by her predecessor, into the big house on Wagner Road. From the beginning, Frank Brach spoiled his wife like a doting father. He bought cars for her. After they were married Helen Brach always had at least one pink car, and pink, her favorite color, became the official color of the Brach Candy Company. The lettering of the Brach's logo on the candy packages was offset by a background of shocking solid pink or lavender and pink stripes. The bags and boxes were bright and eye-catching.

The couple passed their leisure time traveling between a Florida penthouse and the Glenview estate and made occasional side trips to New York City and Tappan Lake, Ohio.

If Helen Brach confided in anyone during the years she and

Frank were married, it was the group of friends and relatives in Ohio. Her long-standing girlfriends were impressed that she never forgot them, said Sue Gorisek, a native of southeastern Ohio, who, in 1978, interviewed a number of women for an article that appeared in *Ohio Magazine*. Margaretta Besozzi of Urichsville told Gorisek, "People said she would change with all that money, but she never did. When she'd come down, we'd sit up all night talking, just like a pajama party." Maybelle Thomas, who, with her husband Spade, took care of Walter Vorhees and the houses and grounds at Tappan Lake, explained to Gorisek, "We were as close as sisters. When they stayed next door she would come over most mornings in her robe and slippers. We'd have coffee, and we'd talk." Helen Brach, Gorisek reported, told Maybelle that she had an "arrangement" with Frank Brach: "sex, but not too often."

While his wife was pouring her heart out to her old girlfriends, Frank supposedly impressed the townspeople with his good humor and folksiness. "Old Frank Brach cut a fine figure on those visits," Gorisek wrote. "Tall and thin with white hair and a neat moustache, he would stroll those quiet main streets, pockets bulging with Brach candies to pass out to delighted children. He would stop at Coultrap's Market near Tappan Lake and head straight for the rack where the Brach candies were displayed. 'Good stuff you've got there,' he would tell Mrs. Coultrap. 'Selling all right, is it?'

" 'Folks around here liked him,' Charles Vorhees said of his brother-in-law. 'He never forgot he was a poor man once.' "

Something about this image of Helen the blabbermouth and Frank as Santa Claus does not ring true. Helen Brach could be direct when she spoke, but she often opted not to. The few Glenview people who had to deal with her found that she preferred to let her money do the talking. As to Charles Vorhees's remarks about Frank, Frank Brach was never poor. When he was a child the Brach family was comfortable, and when he was a teenager they became filthy rich. His associates in Chicago painted less glowing pictures of Frank's disposition. At the end of his life he was most often characterized as a mean old man.

In the 1950s, as Frank Brach settled down with the woman he would be with for the rest of his life, he also acquired two faithful employees who would stay with him just as long. Relationships made of loyal service were more important to Mr. Brach than blood ties. Frank hired Jack Matlick, who was then about thirty years old, as his personal chauffeur. And he met Everett Moore, a certified public accountant with Ernst & Ernst. Moore was first assigned to do the corporate income tax work for the E. J. Brach & Sons company, and the individual tax work for Frank Brach, in 1950. Moore left Ernst & Ernst and established his own office in 1965. Frank Brach hired Moore as his personal tax consultant in 1968. When Frank Brach died in 1970 Moore stayed on as tax consultant and financial manager to Helen Brach.

Frank's brother, Edwin Brach, was seventy-seven years old when he died of a heart attack in January 1965. At the time he was visiting his winter home in Tucson, Arizona, though his main residence was at 595 Sheridan Road in Winnetka. Frank Brach was then the sole surviving founder, and the mantle of the family business passed to him. But Frank was already too old and sick to do much with it. In 1966 E. J. Brach & Sons was sold to American Home Products, a huge conglomerate based in Manhattan that owns numerous manufacturing companies, and assigned to the Standard Brands division. American Home had purchased a thriving business. As of 1963, the Brach company offered a complete candy service to stores, as one company spokesman said, "from hard candy to jelly beans." Over the previous ten years Brach's had grown at a rate of 6 percent a year and was still, by far, the largest candy producer in Chicago. Brach's candy had long since gone into the supermarkets. In fact, half of the company's sales were from those outlets; another quarter came through variety chain stores.

The year the company was sold was the same year Helen's mother, Daisy, died at the age of eighty-eight. It must have been an unhappy time for Mr. & Mrs. Brach.

Frank Brach was very ill and a semi-invalid during the last

years of his life. Some maintain he was senile. He spent much of his time at the Glenview estate, close to the finest doctors and the best hospitals. One community resident remembered the way the local authorities took care of him. For instance, there was a story that he once drove off in one of the Cadillacs and forgot where he was going. The police found him and took him home. At the end of his life Frank was in a wheelchair and depended on Jack Matlick, who had assumed the duties as part-time nurse and valet, as well as chauffeur.

Despite what June Brach had had to say about the close filial bond between Frank and his kids, that may have been an overstatement. When he grew old it was impossible to say what his relationship with his children was. It was known that Frank Brach, Jr., who had married, divorced, and remarried, lived in California quite a bit. The son had not gone into the family business, but then, none of that generation of Brachs had gone into the business. According to the records from his divorce in 1958, Frank, Jr., was not the wealthy man his father was, though he was comfortable enough to provide $175 a month for the wife and two children he was accused of deserting in the late 1950s. Frank, Jr., died when he was fifty-two years old, about a year before his father.

Joyce Brach lived near Helen and Frank. Her first husband was a member of another wealthy North Shore clan, the DeLagos, and the couple stayed on family territory. Joyce divorced and married again, but she never lived farther from Chicago than southern Wisconsin.

Frank Brach was eighty years old when he died on January 19, 1970. Because he was under a doctor's care and the services were private, the press missed the death. Oddly, there was none of the publicity that usually goes with the death of a well-known, prosperous local businessman, no lengthy obituaries like there had been when Frank's father and brother died. Nonetheless, he was buried in style. One Chicago reporter who claimed to have seen the bill from a funeral home for Frank's burial said it struck him as outrageously expensive—in the tens of thousands of dollars.

Frank's will, dated July 1968, left $40,000 to Helen's brother, Charles; $5,000 to Frank's sister, Anna; $3,000 to a cousin Agnes; and $10,000 to his secretary. Frank had also designed trust funds for his son and his daughter. Helen Brach got all the cars, furnishings, clothing, and antiques, plus 60 percent of the value of the adjusted gross of everything else—mostly stocks and real estate. At the time her piece was worth roughly $20 million. As stipulated in the will, the Helen Vorhees Brach Trust was formed, and Mrs. Brach was given the right to take money from the principal any time she asked for it in writing. The widow received all the income from the trust. Anything left, Frank Brach had stipulated, should go to Northwestern Memorial Hospital, the American Cancer Society, and the Chicago Heart Association. Because Frank, Jr., died after the will was made, his money went to these charities. A codicil to the will made in March 1969 canceled the bequest to the secretary.

After Frank Brach's death Helen Brach fired Jack Matlick. They allegedly parted on amicable terms. He had been her husband's servant, and she had no work for him. A few months later, Matlick claimed, he returned and said he had been unable to find another job. Thus he became, by his own definition, her houseman and trusted companion.

6

Mrs. Brach and the Animals

HELEN Brach had a consuming and almost boundless love for animals. Her creatures gave her the affection she craved, and she returned that kindness and provided a lavish lifestyle: the finest food and a run of the house and grounds at Glenview. In 1970, after Frank Brach was buried in Ohio, the widow went to the Bahamas on a vacation. While she was there she received word that her dog Candy, one of several mutts, was dying of a kidney disease. When she was unable to get a commercial flight immediately, she chartered a plane so she could be at the bedside of the sick hound. Candy was buried in a plush coffin with a satin lining, after her devoted mistress gave her a proper wake at a local funeral home.

Half a dozen wildlife foundations and animal welfare organizations, including the Associated Humane Society, the Animal Welfare League, Friends of Animals, and Pet Rescue, were regularly given annual donations from Mrs. Brach. But Helen Brach was the most generous with the Animal Protective Institute, a California-based organization headed by a middle-aged entrepreneur, Belton Mouras. Their closest association came when they were trying to protect the stray dogs of Harrison County. Mouras manned the front line of the battle with the Ohio officials, using Mrs. Brach's money to ferret out the corruption and muster others to the cause. Helen Brach preferred to remain behind the scenes.

The heiress had become a member of the API after she saw a newspaper advertisement about animals in trouble and the work the organization was trying to do. She dashed off a check to the institute. In the space for figures she wrote "$500.00," but on the line below she wrote "five dollars." Mouras wrote her a note asking for clarification. After that she made several more substantial contributions and piqued Mouras's interest in her. In a book he wrote in 1977, titled *I Care About Animals,* an account of his experiences in the animal welfare business, Belton Mouras devoted an entire chapter to Helen Brach and Kim Novak, two heroines to animals. In it he described how he became curious about Mrs. Brach. He had come to realize through his work that oftentimes donors were aware of incidents of animal abuse in their own communities and were anxious to pass on information to the API about work they felt should be done. For this reason, Mouras would seek out his benefactors.

The head of the API made several attempts to meet Mrs. Brach in Chicago; Tappan Lake, Ohio; and Fort Lauderdale, Florida; but these meetings were always cancelled by her at the last minute.

Months went by and Mouras learned more about Mrs. Brach. She had been a heavy contributor to several animal welfare organizations, and she was quite sensitive to abuses in her own area. When Mouras and Brach finally met in Chicago he was impressed by her quiet, direct approach and her candid way of addressing issues that were important to her. Mouras found her inspiring and very angry—angry about the attitude in Harrison County toward the problems of pets and angry in a specific way with the officials of the Ohio dog pound. She was determined to fight the abuse and indifference in the community.

Helen Brach, Mouras said, was wealthy and sophisticated and had been around enough to know that the squalor and brutality of the dog pound near Cadiz, Ohio, was unnecessary and atypical. Publicly run dog pounds could be run in much more humane ways, Mrs. Brach was sure.

Helen Brach was correct in her assessment of the situation at the Harrison County pound; the conditions there were very substandard. The environment had become so horrible partly because of the regional bias against strays that, in a way, condoned the ill treatment of the dogs. When the economy in southeastern Ohio depended on raising sheep—150 years before the controversy arose—laws had been enacted for strict control of the animals who preyed on the livestock. A penalty had to be paid by the local pound to the sheep owner for every animal killed by a roving dog. This law cost the taxpayers in Harrison County several thousand dollars each year, even in the 1970s.

During the spring of 1974 rumors reached Mrs. Brach about the pound and a phony deal involving the local dogcatcher and a kennel owner. She put a private detective on the case and found out that the dogcatcher was selling live dogs from the Harrison County pound to the kennel owner, who was reselling them to laboratories to be used as guinea pigs in scientific experiments. Next, Helen Brach hired some legal talent and had the kennel temporarily closed. Cleaning up the Harrison County pound was a more difficult task, however, and she enlisted Mouras's help to do that. Together they founded the Harrison County Citizens' Animal Protection Society (CAP). The following August representatives from the new coalition—Helen Brach and five other local women—met with the Harrison County Board of Commissioners.

"Some of the points discussed included fees charged when a dog is brought to or taken from the pound, money available from the county's general fund for dog pound use, number of weeks dogs should be kept in the pound while volunteers are looking for adequate homes, lack of an adequate water supply at the pound and methods of alleviating this problem, the possibility of providing separate units to house ill dogs, and the use of a lawn mower at the pound," the *Harrison News-Herald* reported. At that meeting the county commissioners suggested that the CAP people take over the pound's maintenance. Commissioner Edwin Springer told the organizers: "If you are a chartered organization, why can't we just make a contract with you to take care of the dogs? We will pay $40 a month, the same amount we paid the firm which took the dogs for scientific experiments, and you can find homes for the dogs or dispose of them however you want." A modified version of this plan did go into effect for a while, several months later.

In September Mouras sent a team of investigators in to examine the dog pound and make recommendations. A mild and fairly gracious letter to the commissioners followed that visit. It said in part:

> During the course of our survey we found some infractions of the Ohio State statutes. We concluded that the infractions were minor, unintentional, and in most cases either unavoidable or done under mitigating circumstances. We did not pursue allegations of unethical practices, nor did we examine official records.
>
> We understand that Harrison County does not have funds to replace the pound recently ordered closed. Accordingly, if you find our recommendations acceptable we are prepared to immediately pursue the needs of Harrison County citizens. Also, funding for euthanasia, food and veterinarian medical care for animals impounded or gifted to the shelter which the county could not provide can also be arranged.

This was Mrs. Brach's way of saying, through Belton Mouras, that she was willing to build a free animal shelter for the county. At first, the county officials were slow to acknowledge Mrs. Brach's offer. In the meantime the CAP group was chartered and incorporated and given nonprofit status. Members were allowed into the dog pound and were able to build doghouses and feeding troughs and set up a place where the dogs could get shade. They also took over the disposal of dogs that could not be given away and contracted with a local vet, who would handle the matter with injections of painless drugs.

Negotiations between Belton Mouras's delegation and the county officials began in late 1975, but by 1976 the planning committee reached an impasse. The Ohio authorities complained that Belton Mouras and Helen Brach wanted too much control over the project. Commissioner Dwain Smith said, "We can't allow county government to be dictated by the mere whim of a private citizen. We refused to submit to her requirements, which changed constantly."

According to Belton Mouras, Howard Fulton, the man who the commissioners had hired as dogcatcher, was the problem. The CAP members felt that he was sadistic and unreasonable and they would be unable to work with him. Mouras described him as a caricature of a dogcatcher—a violent, aggressive man bent on brutalizing animals and causing trouble for people who would like to help them. Margaret Campbell, a local woman who had become president of CAP, said that after Fulton arrived she and her volunteers were no longer allowed to come in and feed and water the puppies. It was during this rift over the proposed shelter that the Harrison County commissioners broke off the agreement with CAP that had given the animal welfare organization members the responsibility for disposing of the dogs. The commissioners made a new deal with Kiser Kennels of Carollton, Ohio, to make the disposals.

Emotions swelled as the fighting reached new levels. There were harsh words and accusations from both sides at public meetings and in the press. And the paranoia grew. The townspeople gossiped about smear tactics and tricks on the part of CAP members as well as county officials. Helen Brach stayed mostly in the background, where she made enemies as well as friends.

Carol Ledfors, who had become one of Mrs. Brach's friends, was very active, and some people accused her of being the heiress's mouthpiece.

Mrs. Ledfors and her husband, Bob, were indisputably devoted to animals, but it was Carol Ledfors who first caught the public's attention when she began showing up at the commissioner's meetings. On one occasion she presented the board with a picture of a puppy that had been shot and charged that the shooting was illegal. The commissioners said that Howard Fulton had shot the dog, which the dogcatcher contended had mange, when it had gotten loose and he had been unable to catch it.

Another time Mrs. Ledfors brought in a series of pictures showing the gradual deterioration of a dead dog lying on the pound premises over a period of nine days. The decay was terrible, and toward the end the photos showed rats and maggots. In answer to the accusation that he had allowed this to happen, Fulton replied: "I'm sure to this day that they [the animal lovers] planted that dog. Nobody knew about that dog but them."

As the controversies over the dogcatcher, the pound, and the proposed new shelter peaked in the summer of 1976, Mrs. Brach telephoned Carol Ledfors almost every day and often visited the couple at their home in Cadiz, Ohio. "Her big Lincoln Continental would cause some comment because we don't have much of that kind of traffic here," Mr. Ledfors told a reporter. "But, other than that, you'd never know she was rich. She mingled with the common working folks."

Then the winter came and Helen Brach was gone, never to return. Some of the CAP members wondered aloud if these people who seemed to place so little value on animal life placed any value on human life. They wondered how evil men who would shoot down defenseless puppies could be to a person who annoyed them. Evil enough to . . . ?

In his version of the Harrison County story, Belton Mouras rambled at length about small-town politics in general and Howard Fulton in particular. As it turned out, Mouras said, Helen Brach was stopped from building the animal shelter that she wanted to build, but that would not be the end of the story. The day would come, he promised, when the officials in Harrison County would learn to respect the rights of animals.

The people, Mouras hoped, would force their elected officials to mend their ways. He explained that a court had declared that the county was acting illegally in its method of disposing of live dogs. But the Harrison County officials came up with a new scheme even more horrible than the original program. The new plan was entirely legal, though it was in blatant violation of the spirit of the court order. The commissioners contracted with a dog dealer who would come into the pound, kill the dogs there, and then remove the dead animals. The law, Mouras wrote, could not provide protection for dogs that were already dead.

Mouras went on to say that the citizens against animal abuse in Harrison County would not give up despite all the dirty tricks that had been used to try to stop them. CAP members had been able to see to it that conditions at the pound improved slightly since their battle against the authorities began. Also, Mouras emphasized, the group was determined to continue the fight until the bitter end when, he predicted, they would triumph over the narrow-mindedness of small-town politics.

After his book was completed, Mouras went back and wrote a few sentences about the disappearance of Mrs. Brach. He said that she was seen for the last time on February 21, 1977, and added that her mysterious disappearance did not seem to have anything to do with her work for pet welfare. Personally, Mouras said, he was sure that there was no connection between her love of animals and whatever may have happened to her.

For at least a year after Helen Brach vanished, Carol Ledfors continued to write newsy letters to her. She said she believed in her heart that Mrs. Brach was still alive.

PART II

THE INVESTIGATION

7

Helen Brach Is Missing

AFTER he filed the missing person report with the Glenview police, Charles Vorhees returned to Hopedale. At that time, he later told the press, he believed Jack Matlick's version of what happened the weekend before his sister departed for Florida. Vorhees felt sorry for the houseman, he said, because he himself had had to endure the same kind of suspicious questions and innuendos that Jack Matlick was suffering. When Charles Vorhees reported his sister missing, the authorities had been quick to note that he was her legal heir.

Mr. Vorhees had his own ideas about who may have been responsible for Helen Brach's fate, though he did not verbalize them until months after the investigation was under way. He told a reporter that he was angry with the accountant, Everett Moore, and implied that Moore may have been in league with Belton Mouras and the Animal Protective Institute by saying that, immediately after his sister's disappearance, "Moore was after me to keep up Helen's contribution of $100,000 a year to the Animal Protective Institute."

Persons close to the investigation at that time thought that

Belton Mouras may have had something to gain by Mrs. Brach's death. Helen Brach had always been more generous to the Animal Protective Institute than to any other single person or organization. Perhaps she would be at least as benevolent in her will. And, after all, it had been the combined pressure of Everett Moore and Belton Mouras on Jack Matlick which had prompted the investigation into Mrs. Brach's whereabouts in the first place. The tenacious Mr. Mouras, who had been waiting impatiently for the expected annual donation, was pestering both Everett Moore and Jack Matlick with telephone calls from California, trying to get in touch with Mrs. Brach. The Animal Protective Institute was planning to build a new headquarters, and it could not get started without the large contribution Mouras said she had promised.

In late February 1977, the API founder was watching television and saw a Chicago-area private eye named Ernie Rizzo appearing as a guest on "Kup's Show," then televised nationally on NBC. Mouras called Irv Kupcinet, a gossip columnist for the Chicago *Sun-Times* as well as the talk show's host, and asked to be put on to Rizzo. Kup agreed to help Mouras find Ernie Rizzo as long as he would be given exclusive bulletins on any news that developed from Rizzo's investigation. In his column of March 22, Irv Kupcinet was the first reporter to disclose to the world that Helen Vorhees Brach was missing.

Ernie Rizzo, who was thirty-six years old at the time of the investigation, was an ex–Franklin Park police officer who had already made quite a name for himself around Chicago as a private detective. Rizzo's clients were often affluent and influential people, and several of his cases had been well publicized: Charles Walgreen III, owner of a large chain of drugstores, hired Rizzo to shadow his wife Donna. Around the time of the Brach disappearance, Rizzo had uncovered a plot by the wife of a wealthy commodities broker and her state trooper boyfriend to kill the woman's husband. Rizzo had appeared on "Kup's Show" along with Cecil Saxby, the

Scotland Yard detective who solved the Great Train Robbery, and Frank Otash, a Los Angeles investigator who had worked for the late Howard Hughes. Rizzo made an excellent guest. He was a good-looking young man, tall and slender with big eyes and curly brown hair; he was a student of human nature who solved cases by formulating theories about what may have happened and pursuing the evidence to substantiate them. He was never afraid to give his opinion, enjoyed the limelight, and was on a first-name basis with a number of Chicago reporters.

Rizzo was intrigued by Helen Brach, and what was more, he told reporters, Belton Mouras was paying him $1,000 per day. Having served as a suburban cop himself, Rizzo was familiar with the constraints the Glenview police worked under, and he was able to extract information more successfully through various ruses and a few quasilegal methods. This put him at odds with the police. Furthermore, Rizzo gave much of his information to the press.

One afternoon, Ernie Rizzo recalled, he was leaving a building where he had just obtained some important information about Mrs. Brach's activities immediately prior to her disappearance. Sergeant Baumann was just arriving at the location, and Rizzo presumed he was trying to get the same facts and figures. Rizzo imagined that the police were not amused when they read about *his* ongoing investigation in the newspapers.

Soon after the announcement that Mrs. Brach was gone, the sightings began. They said they saw her in Chicago, in Ft. Lauderdale, and in Ohio. One Harrison County woman reportedly spotted Helen Brach in a local supermarket. Another Cadiz, Ohio, resident thought she had seen her in a parking lot. (Mrs. Brach had last visited her Tappan Lake house with Jack Matlick in January 1977.)

Ernie Rizzo had not been on the case very long when he decided to fly to Ft. Lauderdale. He had correctly ascertained that the Glenview police had stayed on their own turf. Though the local authorities had been contacted, no real investigation was under way in Florida. On the doorknob of the Brach condominium, Rizzo found a notice from the telephone company. An installer had come to put in the phone but had found no one there. Then, Rizzo said, he tried the door and it opened, so he went inside. The place was empty except for some packages that had arrived in the mail from Rochester, Minnesota. When the investigator opened them he saw that they contained items from a bath shop at the arcade near the Mayo Clinic. He then flew to Rochester, where he interviewed Phyliss Redalen, the salesclerk at the store, and found a cabdriver who thought he had taken Helen Brach to the airport. By the time he came back to Chicago, Rizzo was convinced that she had flown back from Minnesota on schedule but, once home, had never left Glenview alive. Though he subsequently tried several other theories, Rizzo was convinced that Matlick was lying and that Matlick was the key to the mystery.

Douglas and Adalene Stevens, the Brachs' friends in Ft. Lauderdale, proved to be the best source of information once the Helen Brach hunt began in earnest in March 1977. Mr. Stevens said that Mrs. Brach had told him about meeting someone in a New York hotel where she had been staying over the New Year's holiday, who could arrange an appointment with Dr. Ivo Pitanguy, a plastic surgeon in Rio de Janeiro. It was thought that perhaps she had flown secretly to Rio, though Doug Stevens said she had not made any definite plans that he knew about. "She said she and the man got to talking about cosmetic surgery, and he offered to arrange an appointment for her. She asked us things such as how long it would take to fly to Rio and whether we could go with her. She's not the adventurous type. I don't think she'd ever go to a foreign country alone, but she is the kind of person who'd want to keep it a secret if she were having a facelift."

The Rio excursion sounded plausible for about twenty-four hours, until reporters were able to reach Dr. Pitanguy's secretary, who assured them that Helen Brach had not checked in and had no appointment scheduled. Again, the possibility that she had used an assumed name was considered, but it seemed unlikely that she had gone to Rio at all, especially to Chief Bartlett. He pointed out that, if she was in Rio, she was there without her passport since he had found that when he searched the house.

By the end of March, Rizzo's name was all over the newspapers. Rizzo had linked Richard Bailey, the South American surgeon, and a "mystery man" to form his first what-happened-to-Helen-Brach theory. Rizzo said that Matlick told him that Mrs. Brach had spent the entire day with a mystery man the Sunday before she disappeared. This unidentified person, he speculated, may have been the same man she met in New York the previous New Year's. Mrs. Brach had gone to New York to attend Guy Lombardo's party at the Waldorf-Astoria with her friend Bailey, Rizzo explained. After the party, Bailey returned home to Chicago and Helen Brach remained in New York City, where she met with the mystery man. What this all added up to in Rizzo's mind was that Helen Brach was traveling abroad and "living it up" with the "mystery man."

"They talked about going down to Rio de Janeiro. The carnival down there started the day she left, so you never know. By the time the checks filter back through the banks, a month could have gone by anyway. And if she's with that fellow she met at the Waldorf, he's probably picking up the tab."

The Glenview police were stymied. Matlick had said all he was going to say. They could not find the so-called mystery man, and Richard Bailey refused to talk with anyone. The neighbors did not know anything, and neither did Mrs. Brach's few friends and acquaintances. There was no physical evidence that anything had happened, let alone a murder.

"She was a quiet, conservative, considerate woman," Bartlett said. "She was a bit reclusive—she had few close friends here.

Her neighbors didn't even know her. But she had no history of lengthy disappearances, of eccentricities of that sort."

The psychics had joined the number of speculators guessing where Mrs. Brach was, and both the Glenview police and Ernie Rizzo were contacted. "Almost all the mystics 'see' Helen Brach alive someplace. One says she had an operation that didn't go right, and is hiding. Another says she was the victim of a plot that went wrong. One said he's sure she's being held in Toronto," the private eye told reporters.

Ernie Rizzo is generally given credit for the "meat grinder theory," that Matlick had disposed of Helen Brach's body by feeding it to her dogs, though he later said that the story had gotten all out of proportion. After he learned that Matlick had called five Marshall Field outlets the weekend before Mrs. Brach was said to have vanished, he questioned a salesclerk at the fifth store, who told him that Matlick had purchased a meat-grinding attachment for Mrs. Brach's blender. Everett Moore told Rizzo that Matlick might have wanted an item like that to grind up meat for her dogs. "When Mrs. Brach disappeared back in February the ground was frozen hard as a rock. So was the lake. So if she had met with foul play, I wondered what could have become of her. Then this business with the meat grinder came up. And Moore mentioned ground meat for the dogs, . . ." Rizzo said. "Well, it's too bizarre to even think about. Except that this whole case is bizarre. So you can't ignore anything."

Chief Bartlett found the whole idea outrageous and called the theory, "creative journalism." The three dogs, who had been portrayed in the press as a trio of large German shepherds, were, in fact, three mutts. Luvey, Tinkerbelle, and Beauty were not very large, and they certainly were not ferocious. But even if the mutts had been man-eaters, many believe that a meat-grinding attachment for a blender would not have nearly the capacity for such a job.

Police Chief Bartlett was convinced from the start that Mrs. Brach had, as they say, been a victim of foul play, though she had not been kidnapped. And Bartlett was skeptical about Matlick's story. The police chief finally admitted to reporters that the results from the handyman's polygraph tests were "not very favorable on a couple of questions," though Matlick "still insists he's telling the truth."

A month after the investigation started, Sergeant Baumann said, the Glenview police forwarded their reports to the Cook County State's Attorney's office, then run by Bernard Carey, "because of the amount of money involved." The matter was fast becoming the hottest potato in town. Already there had been some griping by members of the Village of Glenview's board about the time and trouble being spent on *one* Glenview citizen, even though she was a very prominent citizen. The police department, after all, was operating on a limited budget.

When the Cook County Grand Jury started its inquiry into the curious matter of Helen Brach on a Monday morning at the end of April, Kenneth Gillis, the deputy state's attorney assigned to the case, issued subpoenas for Mrs. Brach's financial records—charge accounts and bank statements. He hoped to be able to trace her movements since her disappearance through those records and at the same time check to see if any money was missing from anywhere. Gillis was assuming that Mrs. Brach's disappearance had something to do with her millions.

8

Continental Bank vs. Helen Brach

It was the middle of July 1977, before there was anything new to report in the mysterious matter of Helen Brach, and the bit of information from the Cook County Grand Jury barely qualified as news. John Lewis, an assistant state's attorney, obtained a court order to get into Mrs. Brach's two safe deposit boxes. Along with John Conway, an attorney representing Everett Moore, Moore himself, and Chief Bartlett, Lewis spent a morning opening them. The first box was in the name of both Helen Brach and Jack Matlick. The other was in Mrs. Brach's name alone.

None of the principal characters in this drama had any revelations for reporters on this matter. Attorney John Conway merely told reporters that there were "articles of considerable value," in the two boxes. Helen Brach was known to have some jewelry and, judging from the fact that the safe deposit boxes were never mentioned again, the authorities were obviously satisfied that the jewelry was intact in the boxes.

Beyond that Grand Jury probe, no criminal court ever

looked into the disappearance of Helen Brach. Instead, the investigation that took place did so under the aegis of a civil court proceeding involving Helen Brach's money.

The day after the safe deposit boxes were opened, the newspapers reported that Continental Illinois Bank and Trust Co. had filed a lawsuit asking for permission to hire a private detective to try to find Helen Brach. Accounts said that the twenty-five-page lawsuit was asking to spend as much as $50,000 to find her—the money to come from the income of the trust managed by the bank.

The lawsuit was far more complex than the press had described. By disappearing, Mrs. Brach had abdicated her legal responsibilities to her fortune and created a financial tangle that would take years to straighten out.

Everett Moore, who was, in effect, the comptroller of Helen Brach's business, was the first person to bring the matter of her disappearance to court in the spring of 1977. Moore went to the probate division, before Judge Walter Dahl, and asked that he be designated Helen Brach's official representative for the time being. While Mrs. Brach was alive Moore had handled all her money. Her bills from credit card companies, department stores, and staff members were all sent to him; he paid with checks written on an account at the Continental Illinois Bank, where the trust income was held. (Mrs. Brach had a small checking account in Glenview, which she took care of herself.) Now that Mrs. Brach was missing, Moore wanted the court to name him "administrator to collect," officially giving him the right to do just what he had always done before his employer vanished. Judge Dahl agreed with Mr. Moore. Now Moore had the authority to press forgery charges against Jack Matlick or, at least, to expel the caretaker from the Glenview estate. But Moore did not take any action.

The Continental Bank, however, was not convinced that the bank itself, or Mr. Moore, had the legal right to continue business as usual in the absence of Helen Brach. Continental was a cotrustee with Helen Brach of the Helen Vorhees Brach

Trust set up under Frank V. Brach's will; the bank would be responsible if that fund were mismanaged in the absence of the cotrustee. Originally, Mrs. Brach and Continental were also responsible for two other trusts created by Frank's will: one for Joyce Wartmann Brach, Frank's daughter, and a residuary trust that made gifts to Northwestern Memorial Hospital, the American Cancer Society, and the Chicago Heart Association. (Helen Brach had resigned as trustee of Frank's daughter's trust in 1976.) Because of all this, Continental Bank felt it had an obligation to quite a number of people who might be interested in getting at some of Helen Brach's estate if she turned up dead without having left a proper will. The bank wanted the court to clarify its position so it would be on firm legal ground with regard to Mrs. Brach's trust.

Specifically, since Helen Brach was failing to execute her duties as trustee of her own trust fund, Continental wanted the power to be the sole trustee. It seemed that the bank had that right. Article Five of Frank's will said that "if my wife fails or ceases to act as trustee hereunder, no successor to her shall be appointed and the corporate trustee shall be sole trustee." The property at the time consisted of some $7,800,000 worth of stock in the form of 275,000 shares of American Home Products, the company that had purchased the Brach candy company when Frank retired.

The stock had never been diversified because Helen had always insisted that it be retained. The bank thought it was in her estate's best interest—and thus its obligation—to diversify. Everett Moore thought diversification would go against her wishes. Moore and Continental also disagreed about the income on the trust, which amounted to about $300,000 per year, paid in quarterly dividends. The bank thought it should invest the money for her, and Moore thought he should invest the money for her. If she was alive, Moore was right. If she was dead, the bank was right.

The trouble was that no one knew whether Helen Brach was alive or dead.

Because of this mystery, because the Glenview police had

failed to find her, and because Everett Moore—the bank said—had not even tried, Continental also wanted permission to hire a private investigator and pay for his services out of the principal of the trust.

To clarify these matters, and to flush out any other potential problems, Continental went before Judge George Schaller of the Chancery Division in July and sued everybody who might conceivably be involved. Of course, the bank sued Helen Brach. It sued Everett Moore. It sued Charles Vorhees. It sued the charities. It sued Frank's grandsons, Frank V. Brach III of Shreveport, Louisiana, and Brian F. Brach, an incompetent living in Santa Fe, New Mexico, with the conservator of his person and his estate, Jane Farrar Gordon. The bank sued Betty W. Brach of Del Mar, California, Frank's daughter-in-law, and her son, Frederic S. Wilson, who had both been named in the will of Frank Brach Jr. The bank sued itself, as cotrustee of other trusts created by Frank's will, and it sued "Unknown Others."

Serving everybody with papers took some time. In September the answers started coming in. The American Cancer Society said that, if Helen Brach was found to be dead, it had an interest in the Helen Vorhees Brach Trust. Frank Brach Jr.'s two sons said they had insufficient information, but they wanted their legal fees paid by the Helen Brach Trust. Everett Moore answered that a missing person must be presumed alive until the passage of seven years, so the missing person was entitled to receive the trust income until that time. While replies from the long-lost Brachs continued to trickle in, Continental asked for a *guardian ad litem,* that is, a court-appointed representative, for Helen Brach. Moore, who had already been named administrator to collect, opposed that petition, writing in a counterpetition: "In the present case, there is no indication that the interests of Everett H. Moore, individually or as Administrator to Collect, are adverse to the interests of the missing person." On October 4, Continental asked for a temporary restraining order to hold back the income from the estate. Moore opposed the idea, and Judge

Schaller agreed with him. Moore filed again. This time he opposed the diversification of the American Home Products stock, saying that he had the authority from Helen Brach to trade for her account in the securities market, with the single specific exception of American Home Products.

On November 4, Judge Schaller appointed John Cadwalader Menk, a former president of the Chicago Bar Association, as guardian ad litem for Helen Brach and made Arthur Gorov the representative for the Unknown Others. The introduction of the two court-appointed lawyers would inject new life into a drama that was just starting to get stale.

Menk, a crusty old Scotsman who was a longtime legal powerhouse in Chicago, brought enthusiasm to what he saw as the task of finding out what happened to Helen Brach. Menk, who was something of a crime story buff, was also a skilled actor. The big man with white hair and a ruddy complexion could grin broadly or frown menacingly, depending on the tactics the situation called for. Seated behind his imposing desk at his Sears Tower office, where he would take many of the despositions in the case, he could be quite an intimidating and effective questioner.

Arthur Gorov was somewhat different. An athletically built though average-sized man who wore glasses and had a full head of brown hair just beginning to grey, Gorov was at least ten years younger than Menk. He was razor sharp, spoke quickly and directly, and came across as dynamic. A weekend sailor, Gorov seemed to be in constant motion even in the courtroom. Judge George Schaller never said what he had in mind when he put them together, but Menk and Gorov made a great team.

In December Menk and Gorov, whose interests were similar from the outset of the case, went to court and said they believed Helen Brach made a will before she disappeared, that Moore's lawyer, John Conway, had drawn up that will and had a copy, and requested that the document be brought to court.

Menk wrote:

> Assuming Mrs. Brach's disappearance remains unexplained for approximately the next six years, the trust corpus will have earned some several million dollars in dividend income, exclusive of compounded interest. If this income is turned over to Moore as he has requested, it would become part of the general assets of Mrs. Brach's estate and could quite possibly go to persons or institutions other than those Mrs. Brach may have designated in her Will.

Menk also took this opportunity to address the question of the diversification of the trust.

> The GAL [guardian ad litem] is aware that Mrs. Brach, prior to her disappearance, had apparently several times indicated that she wanted to retain all of the American Home Products stock. It appears that this desire had a somewhat sentimental basis for both Mrs. Brach and her late husband. . . . Nonetheless, it seems to the GAL that no prudent investment counselor could now recommend putting all of the corpus of a Trust into one asset . . . it cannot be assumed that Mrs. Brach would forever continue taking this position with regard to economic changes, etc. Menk suggested that Continental Bank be named sole trustee, which would allow them to diversify the stock, and that Continental retain all the income for the time being.

Meanwhile, back at the estate, Jack Matlick was relieved of his job as houseman by Everett Moore and was soon to be removed from the Schaumburg farm. At the end of December, Moore went back to Judge Dahl in the Probate Division and asked that he be authorized to offer a $100,000 reward for information leading to the location of Helen Brach. Permission was granted.

The $100,000 reward was offered "for information leading to the location of" Helen Brach. "Dead or alive" was the implication. Although Moore, as the administrator to collect, was the sole judge of who should get the reward (and he would be the person to decide how the money would be split in case more than one person brought forward information), the original request that the reward be offered had been made by Charles Vorhees. It was then believed that Vorhees was Helen Brach's principal heir.

Howard O. Roos, a private detective who had been hired by Moore, said that the reward was offered because there was such a lack of evidence as to her whereabouts. "Further investigation and interviewing would not produce results," Roos had decided. Hopefully the reward would "flush out the truth and have someone come forward with personal knowledge of this mystery." Reward notices gave a Chicago post office box and a February expiration date.

In a way, the Menk and Gorov team had taken an adversary position to Moore. They wanted the court to look at the will and to turn control of the trust income over to Continental; essentially, they wanted to act on the assumption that Helen Brach was dead. Moore and his lawyer Conway, on the other hand, had to take the opposite side. As Gorov said, any good lawyer would have had to do what Conway was doing. After all, there was always the possibility that Helen Brach would come walking through the door at any minute, demanding to know what this committee of lawyers was doing with her money.

On January 3 of the next year, responding in writing to the request for the will, Conway told Gorov and Menk that they had no business asking for any such document. He said, "Helen Brach is alive, as far as this court is concerned," and might change her will as long as she was alive. Therefore, an attorney-client privilege existed with regard to the will, and he was not showing it to anyone. The two sides fought over the privilege issue in the petitions and counterpetitions they filed during the next several weeks.

Responses began pouring in soon after the reward offer was made public. Glenview Police Chief Bartlett said, "We've received several reports that she's been seen on airplanes, also that she was sighted riding in a luxury Continental Mark V car in Denver, and that she was seen in a nightclub in Ft.

Lauderdale." Bartlett said that one woman who claimed to have seen Helen Brach on an airplane described her as "very crabby."

And the psychics began telephoning. There were about a dozen phone calls that first week of the reward offer from people who believed they could find Helen Brach by telepathic means. "The psychics seem to agree that she is dead, but none of them know where to find her body." The police chief added that none of the reports had led anywhere and he was still without a substantial clue.

Jack Matlick went to John Menk's office in the Sears Tower to answer some questions in early January. Matlick had, since the first days of the investigation, managed to keep away from the press, which now massed in the lobby of the building, waiting to catch a glimpse of him. Matlick wore a parka with the hood pulled over his face and dark wraparound sunglasses to the interview.

Matlick answered most of the questions that were put to him and disclosed under oath that Helen Brach did indeed have a will. Matlick said that he took a copy of Mrs. Brach's will to the Glenview police after she disappeared to prove to them that he was not named and therefore had nothing to gain by her death. Then, he said, he took the document back to the house where he presumed it still was, lying in a drawer. The houseman also said that he and Helen Brach's brother had burned a drawerful of automatic writings and diaries. He was unable to understand the automatic writings, he told Mr. Menk, and he denied having read the diaries, each of which covered a five-year period. "Mr. Matlick stated he did this because Mrs. Brach had instructed him that, if anything ever happened to her, he was to burn her diaries and her writings," Menk said after the deposition.

Matlick went on to say that he wasn't sure what was in the will, but at a glance he thought that the principal beneficiaries were animal welfare groups and Charles Vorhees. "He said the brother would become a millionaire," Menk told reporters.

Matlick confirmed that he had been fired from his job at the Brach home and that he had been ordered to move from the Schaumburg farm "by spring."

There was a hearing in Schaller's courtroom at the Daley Center on January 25. Menk spoke first and said that, if Conway failed to produce the will, "that would mean that for the next six years this court and all counsel would, in effect, play Rip Van Winkle and wait until the time had expired to find out who really was going to get the money." Gorov agreed, saying that the issue before the court was money—about $1 million. Then he raised a crucial point.

"We have another situation, which came to our attention during the deposition of Mr. Matlick," said Gorov.

"That is the caretaker, isn't it?" Schaller asked.

"Yes," Gorov replied. "During that deposition Mr. Matlick testified that he found a will in the house, a copy of a will in the house in Glenview; that he took that will to the police department to show them that he was not named beneficiary in that will; that he then returned that will to its place in the house, in an envelope; put it away; and never saw it again. . . . Now he is no longer in that house, as far as I can determine. The only one in possession of that house is the administrator to collect. . . . Now, I intend to ask, either today or by petition later, the court to ask Mr. Moore to search the house and present that copy of the will, and it becomes even more important to determine if that copy is the same as the copy that Mr. Conway has, because if she shows the possibility of changing her mind, in the will, then the court has to know that too.

"So it becomes very essential that: one, Mr. Conway produce the copy that he has; and two, Mr. Moore be ordered to produce the copy that he has."

Mr. Conway was completely opposed to Gorov and Menk's suggestion. He argued that Helen Brach's will was not relevant to the proceedings. "I don't know if Helen Brach, before her disappearance or after her disappearance or now or even in the future, may amend or modify that will. I have no idea who any beneficiaries or appointees, under what will, will ultimately be determined to be in her will.

". . . The rules of discovery still require that what is sought to be discovered be relevant to the proceedings." Conway argued for a couple more minutes before Judge Schaller called a halt to the discussion.

"I ruled she is alive for seven years until the proof to the contrary comes in . . . ," Schaller said. "Let's not go into any hypotheticals . . . if in fact years down the road it can be proven beyond a reasonable doubt or by a preponderance of the evidence that she was dead during this period, if she is in fact dead, and show preference that she is not entitled to any of the income of this trust."

There were plenty of rumors floating around the Daley Center that day. More than a few people in the courtroom held the private opinion that the attorney-client privilege was a dead issue at this point, because a document that purported to be the will was secretly circulating. Ernie Rizzo said that he had seen a copy of the will by this time. And a couple of reporters may have had copies of what they believed was Helen Brach's last testament.

Everybody was following the same lead—the court was just lagging behind a bit.

Finally Menk said: "We don't know if she left one will, two wills, or what their dates were, whether he [Conway] had a will dated before the one that was found in the house [by Matlick, according to his own testimony] or vice versa; whether or not the people who witnessed those wills will really stand up under questioning as to whether she was competent at that time.

"There are questions that could well be raised there [i.e., regarding her competence], because of her obvious idiosyncrasies relating to automatic writings from the outside world. Should all of these things be buried for six years? This is not a law school seminar, it is real life, and much of that evidence could be totally lost in six years. People do die, go away, who knows what could happen? There has not been one thing said that would indicate that great harm would be done . . . by the production of this will."

In the end Judge Schaller ordered John Conway to produce the will, because, as he said, it was relevant to the case. Any attorney-client privilege that might have existed was waived, he said, and if Conway refused, he would find him in contempt of court. Conway refused. Schaller immediately found him guilty of contempt, fined him $1,000, and ordered him to serve ten days in Cook County Jail. Conway appealed immediately. (Two months would go by before there was a ruling on that appeal.)

Then Gorov asked if Schaller "would entertain an oral motion for an order on Mr. Moore to search the house and produce that document which there has been testimony does exist or did exist in the house—or would you rather I prepare a petition?"

"I think you better come in with some written petitions on this matter," Schaller said. Then he added what they had all been thinking: "From what I have been reading in the newspapers, there are a lot of documents around that house that are being burned and destroyed. I think the state's attorney better get out there. . . ."

Another waiting period for formal petitioning and a ruling on the search question began. Meanwhile, John Menk and Arthur Gorov, as the appointed representatives of Helen Brach and the Unknown Others respectively, were trying to find out what happened the weekend Helen disappeared. Using their rights of discovery in the Continental Bank suit, they had taken the deposition from Jack Matlick and now they also wanted to take depositions from Everett Moore, who never was too keen on the discovery procedure, and Helen's brother. They said they wanted to ask Charles Vorhees more exact questions about the precise location of the documents that had been found in the house and about the documents that were destroyed by Matlick and Vorhees.

On January 27, Gorov and Menk presented their written petition for the search of the house. A month later Judge

Schaller ordered the search. He said that each of the lawyers could bring one assistant. John Conway and Everett Moore were to be there, and the Glenview police could send somebody if they wanted to. "The date and time of said inspection shall be kept confidential so as to avoid the presence of any parties other than those mentioned above," Schaller ordered. Probably the search was not the most closely guarded secret, however. Menk would say later that they were on an Easter egg hunt, that certain items had been placed in the house for them to find. Those items were a copy of the will and a suitcase that seemed to have been the one Helen Brach used on her trip to Rochester, Minnesota.

A year had gone by since Helen Brach's visit to the Mayo Clinic. And not much more was known about what happened to her than had been known the previous March. Most people had come to the conclusion that she was dead. *Chicago Tribune* reporter Bob Enstad said that the fact that she had not called home to check on her three dogs was the most persuasive indication that she was no longer alive.

Chief Bartlett was terribly frustrated. He told Enstad that he wished he knew more about what Helen Brach had been like; then he might be able to figure out a lead. "We don't know anything about her," he said. "She didn't have many friends or associate much. None of the neighbors knew her. We had people who said she was a benevolent person, and we found people who said just the opposite. I get the feeling that the only ones who care about finding her are members of the Glenview Police Department."

9

The Investigation as Conducted by the Officers of the Chancery Division of the Circuit Court of Cook County

THE reward offer was not getting the results it should have. The authorities had no clues, so they decided they would settle for a motive. Money was the obvious reason for someone to harm Helen Brach. In the year since she had vanished, Mrs. Brach's real estate holdings and dividends on stocks had earned her $525,000. For that reason, the will became the focus for the police investigation as well as the focal point of the court proceedings. The investigation and the court proceedings had begun to merge.

Charles Vorhees, whom an Ohio neighbor had described as "a quiet man who was very touchy about his sister," never was too thrilled with the Chicago authorities and lawyers. In late February 1978, the court ordered him to come to Chicago and give a deposition and, though John Menk described Mrs. Brach's brother as a "cooperative witness who answered all our questions," Vorhees did not tell the court very much during the hour-and-a-half interview. The retired railroad man said that it did not matter to him if he was named in the will. But, when he was asked if he would like to have part of the money, he replied, "I would hope I would get a little."

Charles Vorhees made one of his rare statements to the press that day, on his way from the deposition at the Sears Tower. He said he held out hope that his sister was still alive. John Menk appeared before the media and told reporters that Vorhees confirmed Jack Matlick's account of the burning of the diary and automatic writings. The directions to burn the material were written in what he was sure was his sister's hand, Vorhees had testified.

A few days later John Conway and Everett Moore made one final objection to the search. They said it would endanger the security of the home and would violate Helen Brach's privacy. Judge Schaller overruled their petition, and the secret date was set.

The thaw had begun. It was Saturday morning, April Fool's Day, 1978, a little more than thirteen months after Helen Brach's disappearance. Conway, Moore, Menk, Gorov, Baumann, and Bartlett met at Helen Brach's house at ten o'clock. Gorov brought a friend who knew about antiques, and Menk brought a clerk. Menk would be writing the report for the court, and it would be signed by him and Gorov.

The first thing the search party found was the will. The five-page document was in a kitchen cabinet under a six- or seven-foot counter along the side of the room. The will was in an eleven-by-fourteen-inch envelope addressed to Helen Brach. Accountant Everett Moore's name and address were on a sticker in the return address corner. The will was a carbon copy; imprinted in the lower left-hand margin was the name Pretzel, Stouffer, Nolan & Rooney, Chartered, the law firm for which Conway worked. Menk and Gorov turned to Conway with the document and asked him if it was the will. Conway said that it appeared to be "one of the wills."

Upstairs on the second floor, at the extreme southern end of the house, there was a room that looked to have been used for storage. Inside were three or four suitcases. One of them had a paper tag on the handle showing that it had been on a Northwest Airlines flight to Chicago's O'Hare Airport.

The suitcase was partially filled and looked like it was the suitcase Helen Brach allegedly brought back with her from the Mayo Clinic. Inside the elasticized pocket of the bag there were paid receipts from the clinic, from the hotel where Mrs. Brach stayed while at the clinic, and from a store in the arcade. "There were also in the pocket some miscellaneous coins and a packet of twenty-five unused checks," Menk and Gorov's report said. "In the main part of the suitcase there appeared to be several nightgowns and a pair of slippers. Also there was one baggage identification stub."

The report, which was submitted to the court a few days after the search, pointed out that when Menk took Jack Matlick's deposition back in January, Matlick had been very specific about the will. He said he had shown it to the Glenview police to prove that he was not named in it. When Menk asked him if the police kept the will, Matlick said, "No, I returned it to the estate where it belonged."

"And is it there now?"

"As far as I know."

"Where did you put it? In the house?"

"Back where it was."

"Where was that?"

"In her bedroom."

"In what kind of container? Where is it in the bedroom?"

"In the drawer next to her bed."

The Glenview police claimed that Matlick never brought them any will to look at. They had never seen a will, and they had searched the premises before. Mr. Moore had also searched the premises and found nothing. The last person known to have been in the house was Howard O. Roos, the detective. Roos had searched the place on December 12, after Matlick had moved out; he had been there the entire day, though part of the time he was with somebody from the state's attorney's office. The detective made a thorough search, "including examination of every crawl space and attic space . . . and removal of the contents of every drawer and cabinet . . . reviewing every writing discovered in that search." He had found no will.

Another puzzle was the sudden debut of the suitcase that had supposedly gone from Rochester to O'Hare. It had not been found by the Glenview police either. Chief Bartlett told Menk that he had asked Matlick several times about the suitcase Mrs. Brach brought back from Rochester and that Matlick had never given a satisfactory answer.

And then there were those checks. The report said:

> Also of significance is the fact that the packet of unused checks found by the undersigned in said suitcase were numbered 4926 to 4950 on the Glenview bank account of Mrs. Brach. Mrs. Brach had used checks numbered up to 4922 while she was in Rochester, at the Mayo Clinic. In fact, check 4921, dated 2-17-77, the last morning she was in Rochester, was to the Kahler Hotel (opposite Mayo Clinic), and check 4922, also dated 2-17-77, was for her final bill at Mayo Clinic. Checks 4924 and 4925, also dated 2-17-77, were allegedly prepared later that day on Mrs. Brach's typewriter in her Glenview home, supposedly after her return by airplane from Rochester. Then there is a series of at least six more checks, also purporting to have been prepared on 2-17-77 on the typewriter in Glenview, and these checks are numbered 4976 through 4981. These latter checks were found by police and handwriting experts to have been forgeries.
>
> If Mrs. Brach did, in fact, bring the suitcase in question back from Mayo Clinic, why did she not use the next numbered packet of unused checks that she had taken care to take with her to Rochester, and which she supposedly brought back to Glenview with her in the suitcase found by the undersigned?
>
> Your undersigned respectfully suggest that serious questions of veracity are raised which deserve the Court's careful consideration.

John Menk felt the court had been set up, that the will had been left for the lawyers to find in a very deliberate way. After he called the search an Easter egg hunt he remarked, "We were looking for something better . . . an original . . . something signed by Mrs. Brach and more recent than 1974." He candidly stated that the will they found had been left in the kitchen to sidetrack them in their search for a "real" will. The suitcase Menk dismissed as totally phony. "I don't think she ever came back from Rochester. I think that someone planted the suitcase in the house. I don't think the police could have overlooked it."

Of course, the news that the will had been found was in the newspapers long before court was reconvened on Tuesday, at 10:00 A.M., to receive Menk and Gorov's report. The usual group of about seven lawyers was there, with one addition: an attorney named James Leaton, who was representing Charles Vorhees. (Interestingly, Leaton and Everett Moore had adjacent offices in a Wacker Drive office building.) The talk soon turned to the problem that the lawyers were having with the law enforcement agencies, which could not back away from the Helen Brach case fast enough. All of the attorneys claimed to have been in touch with some important team of investigators, and all of them moaned that they were getting no assistance. Leaton said, "My client, as the only blood relative at all, other than his children, has asked me to participate as much as possible in the ongoing investigation, particularly in the attempt to get the . . . FBI interested. . . . Some time ago, within the last year, Mr. Moore and I asked the FBI to intercede. They wouldn't do it for lack of an interstate feature. . . . More recently I inquired if they wouldn't enter the case, and they wouldn't. But now I think it is time that—and I understand that Mr. Conway has now asked the attorney general—or is intending to ask him. . . . In any event, I think Mr. Vorhees should be represented, if nothing more than to satisfy him that everything is being done."

Gorov said: "The FBI and the U.S. attorney have both been sent copies of the reports filed by Mr. Menk and I of our investigation of the house. . . . They have indicated they are reevaluating their position on an interstate question and they will get back to me further."

Then Conway joined in: "I contacted the U.S. attorney March 6; he has been trying to put me in touch with the FBI. . . . Yesterday I met with an FBI agent. The FBI says the determination of whether or not they should take on cases is in the hands of the U.S. attorney's office, and the U.S. attorney's office says that it's in the hands of the FBI."

"That figures," said Judge Schaller.

"It's taken more than a month to get this contact with the agent," Conway added.

"If the government doesn't want to do anything about it, I can't do anything about it," Schaller said. "But we can sure let them know there are problems here and there and a lot to be looked into."

Gorov added that the Cook County state's attorney had been in communication with him.

"None of this has come to Mr. Vorhees or me," Leaton remarked.

Schaller shot back, "Mr. Vorhees wouldn't come near this case."

"That is why I'm here," Leaton answered. "Can there be an order entered that I would be consulted, though, taken in some participation, so I can advise him of things, of what is going on?"

"Well, at the moment I don't know whether anything is going on," Schaller replied. "Gorov and Menk have rendered their report. That phase of it is ended as far as I'm concerned."

Schaller then called on Conway, who said that now that the court had the will, the privilege issue he had fought the judge on was dead. He handed over his copy of the will, as the court had demanded months ago, and asked that the contempt order against him be vacated. Before ruling on that request Schaller called on John Menk.

"This whole matter had lain dormant for months and months. I went to see the state's attorney's office right after I was appointed, and that is back in November. . . . I went to see the Glenview police, and that was—nobody had been out there. Now, all of a sudden, Mr. Vorhees and others are very interested in all this and will help me out. But I think I can move along by myself under this court's guidance. . . ." Menk, like others before him, thought he might be able to solve the mystery. All the lawyers asked that they be provided with a copy of Helen Brach's will. Schaller refused to vacate the contempt order against Conway; he did, however, agree to modify it. Instead of doing time in Cook County Jail, Conway could serve two hours a day for ten days in Judge Schaller's conference room.

According to the now public will, Helen Brach wanted the bulk of her estate to go to the dogs and cats of the world. The main beneficiary was the Helen Brach Foundation, a not-for-profit organization that Mrs. Brach had set up to help needy animals. She also provided a relatively small—$500,000—trust fund for her brother Charles and his family. The will was dated October 15, 1974. There was a codicil to the will in which Helen Brach directed the executor of her estate to buy a $50,000 annuity policy for Jack Matlick with guaranteed payments for ten years. She also directed that the Charles Vorhees Trust be held by the Glenview State Bank instead of Continental Illinois.

Revelation of the contents of the will piqued curiosity about the Helen Brach Foundation, its executors, and benefactors. There was really nothing suspicious about it. The foundation was set up in May 1974, just prior to the dog pound confrontation in Ohio, as a "general not-for-profit corporation." Under the foundation's Illinois charter, it was supposed to be "operated for the prevention of cruelty to animals, and in connection therewith to promote and carry on educational work designed to promote the kind treatment and the avoidance of cruelty to animals."

In its first two years of life the foundation gave $23,000 to the Animal Protective Institute. Orphans of the Storm, a Deerfield, Illinois, group, got $10,000, and the National Anti-Vivisection Society got $4,000. Several other organizations received grants of about $100. Helen Brach, Charles Vorhees, and Everett Moore were the directors of the corporation.

Had someone measured the excitement level in Judge Schaller's courtroom the morning the will was presented, he might have come to the conclusion that this case was about to go somewhere. But public revelation of the will did nothing more than debunk the idea that Helen Brach was murdered for her money. As John Menk told the Judge that day: "The case is like Alice in Wonderland—it just keeps getting curiouser and curiouser."

There was a lot of attention paid to the gift the will intended for Jack Matlick. The bequest allowed him at least $5,000 a year for ten years. If the interest from the insurance annuity grant were invested wisely, Arthur Gorov said, Matlick stood to make as much as $100,000 during that ten-year period.

The only strange twist to the bequest was that Matlick had sworn under oath that he was not named in the will. But, then, nobody knew for sure which version of the will Matlick was talking about. A gift with $100,000 potential was not really worth that much to a man who stood to make more than that from a life working with Helen Brach. Besides his salary, the accommodations at the Schaumburg farm, and various small gifts, Jack Matlick told his lawyer, Merwin Auslander, that Mrs. Brach had promised to send his daughters through college if they agreed to try veterinary medicine.

The Thursday after the weekend house search, the story of the mysterious suspect—an Art Petacque report—appeared in the Chicago *Sun-Times*. The police, he said, had been watching a "prime" suspect for months. So far, they hadn't gotten any results. The newspaper article described the surveillance:

> Investigators even have asked bartenders and waitresses in North Shore taverns and roadhouses frequented by the suspect to listen and watch for incriminating statements and actions, but to no avail.
>
> At one point, authorities noted, the suspect began making remarks about the disappearance in a discussion in a tavern, but apparently became suspicious of the listener and "clammed up" before making any incriminating remarks.

Investigators said they suspect that Mrs. Brach was killed when their suspect became jealous of her beginning to date seriously another man he saw as a potential rival for her affections and her estate.

Petacque was probably talking about a possible Jack Matlick–Richard Bailey rivalry. The story was a sign of the times. Popular thinking about the motive had changed. If Helen Brach had not been murdered for money, she had been murdered for money and *love*.

It had cost plenty of her money to come to that conclusion.

In May the lawyers began filing their petitions for fees and expenses with the court, on behalf of some eighteen defendants. They would file twice more before it was over. Judge Schaller was not especially generous with Helen Brach's money. He gave $40,000 to the law firm that represented the plaintiff, Continental Bank. Menk got about $19,000. Gorov got $17,500. Continental was awarded $2,500 for unusual services to the trust. Charles Vorhees was given traveling expenses. The rest of the petitions were disallowed.

On April 14 Richard Bailey drew some attention when two boys on their way to school spotted two spray-painted messages on Wagner Road near the Brach house in Glenview. One of the messages said, "Richard Bailey knows where Mrs. Brach's body is. Stop him! Please!" The other said, "Bailey killed Brach." Richard Bailey reported that he had found similar markings near his stables in Morton Grove. He later painted over them, feeling they might be bad for business.

The rest of the summer of '78 held a series of miscellaneous routine courtroom proceedings, mostly petitions for money by the lawyers who could not get any. Continental Bank objected to Everett Moore's fees. Moore objected to the fees paid to Gorov and Menk. The disputes were basically the same as they had always been. The lawyers were simply putting their clients' interests forward. Some assumed that Helen Brach was alive, and others assumed that she was dead, though the latter group could never come out and say that legally. At this point Moore wanted the investigation stopped. Gorov and Menk were, in a sense, sleuthing—taking depositions from anybody who might know anything about Helen Brach's whereabouts. But no one else was looking into the matter for them. In August Judge Schaller called Gorov and Menk in and told them to work together to keep their costs down. He might have hoped to wrap up the proceedings by the end of the year, but it was going to take much longer than that. In December 1978 Gorov and Menk asked for a ninety-day extension for discovery proceedings, and Schaller granted it.

Though the substantial part of the investigation was going on in court, the Glenview police occasionally got a lead.

In October the skeleton of a white woman believed to have been in her sixties and appearing to have had greying reddish hair was discovered decomposing in a forest preserve at 159th Street and Wentworth in Thornton Township, near the southern suburb of Calumet City. The body, which seemed to have been dead for months, had no teeth. It was reported at the time that Helen Brach had worn dentures.

During the twenty-four hours subsequent to the discovery of the body it was learned that the clothes found near the dead woman did not match the clothes Jack Matlick had said Helen Brach was wearing when she vanished. The Cook County medical examiner, Dr. Robert Stein, ascertained that the skeleton was the wrong height and structure, and in his statement to the press he added that he had learned that Helen Brach did have most of her teeth.

In commemoration of the second anniversary of Mrs. Brach's disappearance, Bob Enstad wrote a piece about the legal woes of the Animal Protective Institute.

First there was the lawsuit by the California attorney general that charged that API officers had misused $100,000 in charitable contributions. The dispute was settled in 1978. Among other things, the agreement stipulated that the API be made beneficiary of a $40,000 life insurance policy Belton Mouras had taken out on himself and that the API would make a "significant" donation to research in animal birth control.

Belton Mouras's troubles with the IRS started in late 1977 when API's tax-exempt status was revoked. The IRS said that the API, supposedly founded to protect wildlife, was a conduit for fleecing rich widows and that contributions for the organization were used to pay for office expenses, lobbying efforts, and large salaries for people like Belton Mouras, who was making $48,000 back then.

As a result of the revocation of tax-exempt status, Charles Vorhees and Everett Moore agreed that the API would get no money from the Helen Brach Foundation in 1978. By 1979 the API-IRS dispute had made its way up to the Court of Claims in Washington and the API had been temporarily reinstated as a tax-exempt group pending the outcome of the appeal.

When it was revealed that most of Helen Brach's estate would go to the Brach fund for animals, the importance of the API's tax-exempt status was heightened. "If we fail, it would put us in jeopardy of [not] getting her money," Mouras said. "The money will go to the foundation, so we will make our bid. By precedent she knew and favored this organization. She was pleased with our work. We think we will get the money [for a new headquarters building] out of her will."

Everett Moore, in one of his few conversations with a reporter, said, "You can't be giving to an organization that is not tax exempt. The foundation has to give to tax-exempt organizations in order to maintain its own tax-exempt status."

In a conversation with a different reporter, Charles Vorhees sounded more emotional about the situation when he said that he did not want the API to receive any more of his sister's money.

Belton Mouras concluded philosophically that the problem would be settled in probate court whenever Mrs. Brach was found to be physically or legally dead.

10

The Last of the Litigation

ARTHUR Gorov and John Menk decided to ask that another reward be offered; the free information they were getting was not worth much. Early in 1979 they went before Judge Schaller and asked him to authorize a payment of $200,000 from Helen Brach's trust fund for information about her disappearance. Menk wanted a six-month time limit put on this big budget offer. He thought that the two-month $100,000 reward offer made in 1978 might have been inadequate. More money and more time would bring somebody out of the woodwork.

As affable and outspoken as ever, Menk explained that $200,000 was a drop in the bucket under the circumstances. "We are dealing with an estate of over $20 million." In court he told Judge Schaller that to block the reward "would be like attacking motherhood." John Conway did not oppose the idea, but he wondered if doubling the amount might prompt somebody with information to wait in hopes that the ante would be upped again.

On January 31, 1979, Judge Schaller ordered that a reward

of $200,000 be offered for "written information leading to the discovery of the whereabouts of Helen Brach, dead or alive, or the disposition of her body." The reward was to be paid out of the Helen Vorhees Brach Trust, and it was to expire six months later. It was an incredible offer if one thought about it, and yet there were no takers, lending more credence to the theory that, whatever had happened to Helen Brach, money had nothing to do with it.

In February another law firm—Keck, Cushman, Mahin & Cate, representing Helen Brach's animal-welfare foundation—jumped into the fray on behalf of the world's stray pets by filing an appearance with the court. Any further involvement with this case is not reflected in the court files.

In March Arthur Gorov subpoenaed the three women who had witnessed the codicil to Helen Brach's will, hoping that the changes she had made would shed some light on what happened to her. But the three were Glenview Bank employees who had never seen Mrs. Brach before or since. During the first week in April Gorov and Menk petitioned for another 120 days of discovery. Moore opposed the extension, all but accusing them of playing detective at Helen Brach's expense. "The Co-petitioners have participated in these proceedings for fully seventeen months, an extended and more than adequate period," Moore said. Nonetheless, Gorov and Menk were granted the extension.

Other than the spray-painted accusations of Richard Bailey, there had been no developments in almost a year now. Glenview Police Sergeant Joseph Baumann was called in for a deposition, his second in the case, at John Menk's office. Menk wanted to ask him about his investigation of the spray painting. Present for the interview, in addition to Menk and Gorov, were attorneys Richard C. Robin, representing Continental Bank; John Conway, representing Moore; and James Leaton, representing Charles Vorhees. Baumann started by handing over copies of police reports and pictures of the spray paintings. Some of the pictures were taken at Bailey's stables in Morton Grove and some near the Brach house. The messages were basically the same: *Richard Bailey knows where Mrs. Brach's body is. Stop him! Please!* and *Bailey killed Brach.*

Menk asked Baumann about his first knowledge of Richard Bailey. Baumann said that he had gotten Bailey's name from Jack Matlick. Matlick had supposedly told Baumann that Mrs. Brach had gone out with Bailey on the night of February 20, contrary to later reports that Matlick had not known the man she went out with that night. When Baumann asked Bailey about the spray-painted messages, he said, Bailey told him that a stable owner, one whose name had not come up before, had "taken a poke at him or pushed him in regards to some kind of horse deal." Baumann said that he then went to see this stable owner, who indicated that he did take a poke at Bailey, because, in Baumann's words "he . . . felt that . . . Bailey was cheating him out of $25,000 on a horse." But, Baumann said, the irate stable owner told him he had nothing to do with the spray-painted accusations.

Baumann then visited another horseman, Frank Jayne, Jr., at the Northwestern Stables in Morton Grove. "Mr. Jayne stated that he and Mr. Bailey were competitors in the same business, and he didn't like Bailey. He didn't like the way he operated with elderly women, and he felt he was a con man." Baumann said he saw some other horsemen in the course of the investigation, all supposedly associates of Frank Jayne and, according to Bailey, all jealous of Bailey, because he ran a reliable business. Baumann said that Bailey said that "they had threatened to torch his stables."

"After we started getting in a little deeper," Baumann said, "he refused to talk to me any more about it. I stated, 'What are you referring to about being torched?' He said, 'When I talk to my attorney.' He said, 'I don't have to talk to you.' I said, 'That's right. You don't have to talk to me if you don't want to.' And that was it. . . . Oh, I would go to his stables once in a while to see how good his health is. And I [asked] him if he had learned anything more about Mrs. Brach. Being a horseman maybe he would come up with something. I would talk to him and he wouldn't give me any information at all. He'd say he hadn't heard anything."

John Menk asked Baumann about Bailey having taken Mrs. Brach to Guy Lombardo's party at the Waldorf-Astoria in New York the New Year's Eve before she disappeared and about Bailey having made arrangements for her at the Mayo Clinic. "You have to understand one thing," Baumann said. "This information that I'm giving you is just information I got from Jack Matlick. . . . Bailey did admit that he did make arrangements for her to go to Mayo Clinic. I asked him how he could make such quick arrangements." Although Bailey never really answered that question to Baumann's satisfaction, he did corroborate the New Year's Eve date.

When Menk finished with his questions, John Conway asked Baumann about Bailey's relationship with the other horse traders. "Are they simply competitors? Do they sell things to each other?" Conway asked.

"This is a very hard question to answer, Mr. Conway," Baumann began, "because I don't know. They appear to be at each other's throats. But when you do talk to different people around the stables, just inquiring, you know, people tell you they appear to be friends. So it's very hard to answer. If they do any business together, I don't know."

James Leaton was more antagonistic with Baumann than the other attorneys. He asked Baumann if a handwriting expert had ever looked at the spray-painted writings to determine if they were done by one or more people. Leaton was serious. Baumann said he didn't know if that type of thing could be found out. "There was no effort made to find out?" Charles Vorhees's attorney asked.

"There was no conversation with anyone about his [Bailey's] receiving $25,000 from Mrs. Brach to make a purchase in South America?"

"No," Baumann replied.

"Or that he came back without the money or the horse?"

"No."

Baumann reiterated that Jack Matlick told him that Bailey

liked to go out with "old broads." Then he added, "Jayne, Bailey. . . . These are very difficult people to talk to. . . . I could never find P. J. [Bailey's brother]. He travels all over the country, I understand. . . . As far as I know [three of Helen Brach's horses] were taken from Bailey's stables just recently . . . to the Windward Stables in Mundelein. . . . At this time I suppose they are in Florida because I did talk to her horse trainer . . . Pete DeVito at the Arlington Park racetrack, at the stable there. [They were] raced under her name there. . . . In fact, according to what I read in the paper, they were doing pretty good."

Arthur Gorov interrupted Leaton's cross-examination to ask if there was any evidence that Bailey knew anything about Mrs. Brach's being killed. "The only thing I could testify to is that this was written in the street and we tried to ascertain who wrote it. And we have not been able to do this at this time," Baumann replied.

Leaton broke in. He was losing patience. "Are you in charge of the entire investigation for the Glenview Police Department?"

Baumann answered, "Yes."

"Are you familiar with the forged checks? What was done?"

"They were checked by a graphologist from the Continental Bank," Baumann replied. "They were also checked by a handwriting expert from Northern Illinois Crime Lab . . . [who] determined that [the signatures were] not written by Mrs. Brach. . . . They were inconclusive [as to whether they had been written by Matlick]. . . . They never took Mrs. Matlick's handwriting. . . ."

"No relatives, friends, associates?" Leaton wanted to know.

"Never had any friends or associates," the police sergeant answered.

"Well, wasn't there a suggestion of a possibility of a mail fraud charge? Did you contact the post office department?"

Gorov interjected, "This must be the fiftieth time I've heard you talk about the postal authorities."

John Menk put a stop to the bickering when he said that

Baumann had been brought in for questioning about the spray painting and anything else was not their business.

It was springtime again—time for the attorneys to collect their fees. The law firm for Continental Bank was awarded $12,500. Menk got $17,000 and Gorov $13,000. Continental Bank was awarded $1,300 in extra trustee fees.

Richard J. Bailey's name had finally surfaced in a deposition. Though estimates varied, the fifty-year-old horse dealer had dated Helen Brach for four years before she disappeared. Bailey was linked to the Jayne family, a group of show horse owners, who had an outlaw reputation in Chicago. And Bailey was known as a ladies' man. If one was looking for someone with a questionable background, Richard Bailey was made to order. He quickly became, as his lawyer Jo-Anne Wolfson put it, "a major suspect" in the Helen Brach case as far as the news media was concerned. John Menk subpoenaed Bailey for a deposition. Wolfson moved that the subpoena be quashed and that the deposition—if it had to be taken—not be disclosed to reporters. Her client would surely be a victim of character assassination at the hands of the press, Wolfson argued. Both her motions were denied.

Bailey was ordered to show up at the Sears Tower, and when he did on a June day in 1979, a crowd of reporters was waiting for him. Bailey strode to the elevator wordlessly, looking every inch the suburban playboy wearing a blue suit with an open-collared shirt.

John Menk asked Richard Bailey these questions:

> Did you know Mrs. Helen Vorhees Brach? When did you last see Mrs. Brach? Are you involved in a lawsuit as a defendant brought by a Mrs. Karstenson? Do you have a stable known as Bailey Stables on Harms Road? Do you have a brother by the name of P. J. Bailey? Were you instrumental in any way in the sale to Mrs. Brach of a group of racehorses? The 1976 income tax return of Mrs. Brach covering her business activities as a racehorse owner shows that Mrs. Brach acquired on the following dates and for the following prices, these horses: Brach's

The Last of the Litigation 87

Sweet Talk on March 31, 1975, for $22,500; Brach's Vorhees Luv on March 31, 1975, $27,500; Potenciado, purchased on June 30, 1975, for $48,261; on March 30, 1976, Brach's Hilarious, $27,300; and on March 30, 1976, Vorhees Pleasure, $27,300; on March 30, 1976, Vorhees Diplomat, $29,400; on January 19, 1976, Brach's Honesty, $10,500; Brach's Luv, purchased on January 15, 1976, $13,335; on August 25, 1976, Misty JJ for $8,500; on October 2, 1976, Call-the-Turn, $5,000. Did you sell Mrs. Brach any of those horses? Did you know anything about the sale of those horses to Mrs. Brach? Did Mrs. Brach own any racehorses at the time you met her? Where did you meet Mrs. Brach for the first time? Were you with Mrs. Brach on New Year's Eve in December of 1976? Was it your suggestion that Mrs. Brach go to the Mayo Clinic in February, 1977? Do you have any information whatsoever about the whereabouts of Helen Brach? Do you know if she is alive at the present time? Do you have any information of any kind which you think would be of assistance in ascertaining the whereabouts of Helen Brach? Did you report to the Morton Grove police that someone had spray-painted in front of your stables some comment as to Mrs. Brach? Is it a fact that there was spray painting on the road in front of your stables to the effect that Richard Bailey knew where Mrs. Brach's body was buried? Is it a fact that there was spray-painted on Wagner Road in the vicinity of Mrs. Brach's residence wording to the effect that Richard Bailey knew where Mrs. Brach's body was? Is it a fact that a legend to that effect was also inscribed on your car at about the same time? Is it a fact that you told the police that you thought this was the result of a feud between you and some other horsemen? How often during the year 1976 did you see Mrs. Brach? How often during 1975? 1974? 1973? Did you give business advice to Mrs. Brach during the years that you were seeing her? Are you married, sir? Were you married during the time you were seeing Mrs. Brach? When were you last in the Brach residence on Wagner Road in Glenview? Did you telephone Mrs. Brach from Florida while she was in the Mayo Clinic? When Mrs. Karstenson, the lady whose name [was] mentioned before, in the lawsuit . . . was in Mayo Clinic, is it a fact that you went to Mayo Clinic and came home with her the day she was discharged? Did you have dealings in which you sold a number of racehorses to a Mrs. Waldorf? Did you accept jewelry from Mrs. Waldorf in payment of those horses? Were you ever in the Brach residence on Wagner Road? When did you first learn of Mrs. Brach's disappearance? Did you ever talk to Mr. Matlick concerning Mrs. Brach's disappearance? When did you last discuss in any way with Mrs. Brach the purchase of a condominium in Ft. Lauderdale, Florida? When did you last see Mr. Vorhees? Did you go to Mayo Clinic to see Mrs. Brach at any time while she was there in February of 1977? Is Frank Jayne, Jr., a business partner of yours? Were you aware that Mrs. Brach's income tax return showed a loss for the year 1976 of approximately $120,000? What do you know about the Helen Brach Foundation? To your knowledge who are the trustees of the Helen Brach Foundation? Have you ever talked to Belton Mouras of the California organization known as the Animal Protective League? [Menk meant the Animal Protective Institute.] How old are you? Have you ever been known by any other name? Have you ever been convicted of a felony? Have you ever been involved in litigation concerning the sale of racehorses? Did you spend New Year's Eve in December 1975 with Mrs. Brach? Did you ever take Mrs. Brach to dinner? How long before Mrs. Brach went to Mayo Clinic did you leave for Florida? Did you telephone Mrs. Brach from the Colony Hotel in Palm Beach? Did you talk to the police concerning Mrs. Brach's disappearance? Do you know Everett Moore? Do you know that Everett Moore is the administrator to collect the estate of Helen Brach? Where did you first meet Mr. Moore? Did you ever discuss with Mr. Moore the question of Mrs. Brach's disappearance? Did you ever go to Ohio to Mrs. Brach's home there with or without Mrs. Brach? Were you ever charged with anything in connection with the disappearance of Mrs. Brach? Do you have a brother named William Bailey? Does William Bailey have a wife by the name of Shirley Bailey? Did you ever discuss with Mrs. Brach her plans for the Helen Brach Foundation? Did you ever see a document that purported to be a last will of Mrs. Brach? Did you ever see the suitcase that Mrs. Brach took to Mayo Clinic with her? Mr. Bailey, would you give us your business addresses for the last seven years? Home addresses for the last seven years? Have you ever been in any other businesses, other than that of buying and selling horses or operating a stable for horses?"

Everybody involved in the Helen Brach affair would have loved to hear the answers to those questions, but Bailey did not utter a syllable. He invoked the Fifth Amendment on every question, including the one about his address, through his attorney Jo-Anne Wolfson. After John Menk asked each question, Wolfson said that Bailey would not answer because his answer might incriminate him.

When Menk went back to Judge Schaller and asked him to force Bailey to talk, Schaller instructed Wolfson to give some reasons why Bailey had not spoken at all, why she had asserted his Fifth Amendment privilege for him. Judge Schaller added that some of the questions Menk had asked would have in no way incriminated Mr. Bailey. On August 15, Schaller said, he would rule on the question of Richard Bailey's silence.

The second reward offer expired on July 31, 1979. Those who had offered information Menk described as mostly self-styled psychics and would-be investigators who told of scenes they had in visions or gave facts that were already well known and well publicized. Menk theorized that the sources of "good" information were too scared to contact the court. "Quite obviously these people are afraid. If one of these persons gave out information, his life would be in complete jeopardy. They simply can't afford to come forward."

When August 1979 came, Judge Schaller upheld Bailey's constitutional right to maintain his silence. The only thing that was learned from the Bailey exercise, besides the extent of Menk's suspicions, was that Richard Bailey had something to hide.

Finally a deposition was taken of Everett Moore. Moore answered all the questions put to him. His testimony suggested a normal business manager–client relationship. Moore described Helen Brach as he knew her: a healthy, cautious, intelligent woman who would never drop out of sight of her own free will. She was not depressed as far as he could tell, and he did not perceive any changes in her behavior prior to her disappearance.

"Did she ever discuss any particular marriage plans?" John Menk asked. "I could conceive where that might be a financial concern to her, and she might have discussed it with you from, one, a tax angle; from two, a premarital agreement type angle. Something of that nature."

Moore replied: "She never got certainly that serious. If she had gotten that serious about getting married, I think that question would have come up. It never did come up as to what was the effect, if any, between a single person and a married person, tax status, or a premarital agreement or something like that you're referring to. She had not raised that question with me, nor had we discussed it."

The very last statement in the lawsuit was filed in spring 1980. It came from an officer at the Continental Bank who had contacted Helen Brach about a month before she disappeared and urged her to diversify her stock. She told him that she would think it over and talk to him later, he said. On March 1, 1977, he heard she was gone.

It was the summer of 1980, three years and some months after Helen Brach was told to lose a little weight, when Judge Schaller brought the matter to an end. He terminated Menk and Gorov and found that Everett Moore should continue to handle the assets of Helen Brach, including the income from the trust, but not the trust itself, just as though she were alive. Continental Bank was named sole trustee of the Helen Vorhees Brach Trust created by her late husband Frank, and therefore, they could diversify the American Home Products stock if that was what they wished to do.

That order presently sits in the pending files of the Chancery Division of the Circuit Court of Cook County and is the last official word on the subject until February 21, 1984, when Helen Brach can be declared legally dead and the matter can go to probate.

PART III

WHAT HAPPENED

11

The Morris Ferguson Connection

By the summer of 1980, everyone believed that Helen Brach was dead.

Bookkeeper Everett Moore was left with the rather bizarre responsibility of maintaining Mrs. Brach in absentia in the style she had become accustomed to in actuality. The candy heiress had received an income of about $1 million a year since the spring of 1977, and her expenditures had almost equaled that amount. As curator for the Brach estate, Moore hired gardeners, repairmen, snow removal workers, and security guards for the Glenview home. He also maintained the house at Tappan Lake. In both places he paid phone bills, even though the phones were rarely used. A monthly mortgage payment and maintenance dues went to the Florida condominium, and Moore paid upkeep for the Unionport gravesite. Thousands of dollars went to the boarding and veterinary fees for the nine racehorses she owned, and he even kept up a subscription Mrs. Brach had to *Classic* magazine for horse aficionados. It cost $22 each year.

Everett Moore also gave the gifts that he thought Mrs. Brach would have given. In 1979 the Arthritis Foundation received $1,000, Friends of Animals got $100, and the Animal Protective Institute—its tax-exempt status reinstated—received $75,000.

Everyone who believed that Mrs. Brach was dead had his own idea about how she had gotten that way. Soon after the Continental Bank lawsuit ended, it began to emerge that some of the lawyers and police officers involved believed that Helen Brach's demise may have been arranged by a conspiracy. In a carefully worded question-and-answer interview that appeared in the *Chicago Tribune* on May 19, 1980, John Cadwalader Menk described what he thought had happened to Helen Brach to reporter Robert Enstad:

> Enstad: Mr. Menk, you had never known or met Mrs. Brach, but did you get a perspective of her character in your investigation?
>
> Menk: Yes. She was a rather reticent, conservative woman. I think she was a lonely woman. She lived alone in a large house with few close friends or social activities. She did not do any club work—bridge clubs and so on. Her only interest appeared to be animals and animal welfare.
>
> Enstad: Whatever became of her?
>
> Menk: I think that she died within eight or ten hours after leaving Mayo [on Feb. 17, 1977].
>
> Enstad: Where did she die?
>
> Menk: I think it happened somewhere in Minnesota or Wisconsin. Someone she knew or trusted picked her up after she left Mayo. She was the type of person who was extremely reluctant to get involved with strangers.
>
> Enstad: So what happened after she was picked up at the Mayo Clinic?
>
> Menk: Whoever picked her up had confederates waiting on the alleged journey back [to her home in Glenview.] They intercepted her, and that was that. It was a conspiracy.
>
> Enstad: You mean there were hired killers?
>
> Menk: It is possible.

Enstad: You have no idea where all this might have happened?

Menk: No.

Enstad: Investigators have been told that she flew back to Chicago and then went to her Glenview home for a few days before leaving for Florida. Is that right?

Menk: I don't think she came back on that plane. I don't think she ever got back to that house.

Enstad: Assuming she was murdered, why would anyone want to kill her?

Menk: The motive is unclear. It could be fairly complex, considering the size of her estate.

Certainly the motive would seem to involve money, because there has not been the slightest indication that she had any enemies. The exact means by which someone expected to exploit her holdings is not that clear.

Enstad: What, then, is the motive?

Menk: Horses. They really rooked her on the horses. The first so-called race horse she bought, for $45,000, never even finished a race, let alone win anything. She didn't know anything about horses. She had never done anything with the millions Brach had left her—she was very conservative—and then suddenly she gets into this big racing thing. It was out of character for her. She never bet on horses or went to the track.

Enstad: So you think she was talked into buying the horses?

Menk: Who knows? There is no direct evidence.

Enstad: Then how did this horse thing lead to her murder?

Menk: I suspect that by December of 1976, two months before she disappeared, she had had it and could not be conned any longer.

Perhaps Mrs. Brach said to someone there was a lot of funny business going on and this got back to the people who knew about this. To cheat a multimillionaire like Mrs. Brach is another thing. If she blew the whistle, it might lead to an investigation.

Enstad: So they got scared?

Menk: That could be, that they felt they couldn't take a

chance, even though this might not be the biggest reason for killing someone.

Enstad: What happens now?

Menk: It is very difficult to understand why the state's attorney's office had not brought someone before the grand jury and granted them immunity or something. After three years the trail as far as ordinary investigation is concerned, is very cold. So you have no vehicle left, except the grand jury.

What case can you jeopardize? The only alternative is to let the Brach case become a dead file, which I think would be highly unacceptable.

Apparently Charles Vorhees had come to some of the same conclusions as John Menk, because in August, 1980, he directed his attorney, James Leaton, to petition the probate division for another investigation and reward offer. The funds, of course, were to come from Mrs. Brach's income. Vorhees wanted to hire "a substantial detective agency," because, as he said, "If they can spend thousands of dollars [from the estate] for attorney's fees, I don't know why they can't use some to help find her."

When Mr. Leaton went before Judge Henry Budzinski on September 23, 1980, he made it clear that Mrs. Brach's brother had a specific type of probe in mind. Vorhees wanted the detectives he would hire to be directed to find Paul "P. J." Bailey, Richard Bailey's brother, and question him. Leaton told the judge that Richard Bailey was a member of a "cabal of horsemen" from the north suburbs. He said that another member of that group, Silas Jayne, had been convicted of conspiracy to murder his own brother, George Jayne. Vorhees's lawyer rambled on about how the horse traders liked to take advantage of rich widows and said that one woman, who had sued Richard Bailey for $365,000 because she felt he had duped her in a horse deal, had had her barn burned.

Leaton said that "the day following [the fire] Bailey's car was found near the farm, and he was also near the farm." There was a lake on the woman's property, and Leaton said they wanted that lake dragged for Helen Brach's body.

Judge Budzinski told the lawyer that he was tossing around allegations, information that should be handled by the state's attorney's office. The hearing on the petition ended when Budzinski rejected the idea for another investigation and approved a reward offer of $250,000, the largest of its kind in history, that would expire on March 25, 1981.

A few days before the fourth anniversary of Mrs. Brach's disappearance, in February 1981, there was thought to be a major break in the case. Sergeant Baumann called some reporters with whom he had become friendly over the previous four years. He said there was a man serving time in a Mississippi prison who claimed that he had been offered $10,000 to pick up the body of the "candy lady" in a suburb of Rochester, Minnesota, and rebury it in Wisconsin.

Baumann would not reveal any details or the man's name, he said, because he did not want to jeopardize the informant's life or the possibility that criminal charges might be brought.

Days later it was learned that the man was named Morris Ferguson, known in some states as a small-time crook who had spent most of his twenty-nine years in one jail or another. The stories he told about Helen Brach's body changed from day to day and from interviewer to interviewer. He said that he had been paid a sum of money but had decided not to go through with the job of moving the body. He told one investigator that he had actually "moved Miz Brash's bones." In another version of Ferguson's story he said that part of the deal specified that he was to kill Jack Matlick. And he told at least one reporter that he did not know anything about the Helen Brach matter at all.

When Helen Brach disappeared in 1977, Morris Ferguson was in an Illinois prison at Menard serving concurrent sentences for robbery. Sheriff Harvey Tacket of Washington County, Mississippi, said that his records indicated that Ferguson grew up in Greenville, Mississippi, and attended Coleman High School there. Ferguson had been in trouble for theft since he was twelve years old. In 1965 he moved to Chicago, where he continued his career as a thief until 1971, when he landed in Cook County Jail charged with robbery and murder. The murder charge was dropped, but he was convicted of robbery.

In prison Ferguson acquired the nickname "Slab," though there is no evidence to support the notion that he was a killer. In 1976 Ferguson escaped from the Illinois facility and was captured and sentenced to an additional seven to twenty years for a bank robbery he committed in Stoneville, Mississippi. But before he could serve that sentence he was returned to Illinois to finish his original sentence and do an additional one to three years added on for the jailbreak. Somehow Ferguson was paroled from Menard on June 20, 1979. According to one version of his story, he was hired at that time to rebury Mrs. Brach's body.

Ferguson had been out of jail about a month when he was arrested in Leland, Mississippi, on a traffic violation and possession of a concealed weapon. From there he was sent to the Mississippi penitentiary at Parchman to serve two concurrent twelve-year terms for armed robbery.

While at Parchman, Ferguson allegedly began telling his story about Helen Brach, and word eventually reached Sergeant Baumann in Glenview. A rumor floating around at the time said that the word on Ferguson may have come to the Glenview police through Silas Jayne. Baumann told reporters that he had interviewed Ferguson on November 14, 1980, and December 18, 1980, and that the convict was willing to take a lie detector test. The reason that he had not yet administered the test was because he had been busy doing other work on the case.

The alleged plot had an aura of phoniness about it. Ferguson said he was offered the ridiculously low sum of $10,000 to relocate the body. This claimed amount was especially absurd considering that the body was four years old and had a $250,000 bounty on it. The following week, in February, 1981, Baumann told the press, "We're close to an indictment," and went to Mississippi. A polygraph test was administered at Baumann's request, but the results were never reported to the public. Ernie Rizzo, who claimed to have the inside track on what had happened, said that the stickup man did not even know the names of the main characters in the Brach story.

The digging took place at Lake Kegonsa State Park, about fifteen miles southeast of Madison, Wisconsin. The implication made by some of the newspapers was that the authorities dug the seven-by-three-by-three foot hole because Ferguson had told them that was where he had hidden the body.

But there was yet another explanation for the digging at that spot. Two psychics, Reverend George Pettit and Josephine Smith, both from Columbus, Ohio, had "visualized" Helen Brach's body at the site near Madison. Though the Wisconsin police were skeptical about the information, they learned that Pettit was the head of the Psychic Science Institute in Columbus, a legitimate research organization, and when the pair arrived in Wisconsin, traveling at their own expense, the police decided to try their suggestion.

Helen Brach's body was not found in Wisconsin.

In the meantime the Ferguson story had taken another twist when the convict hired an attorney from Sunflower County, Mississippi, Tommy McWilliams. McWilliams was checking Ferguson's story while trying to negotiate the rights to the tale and collect the $250,000 reward. In June 1981, McWilliams made the first of a half dozen trips to the Chicago area, where he talked with police and various media organizations.

According to the Pioneer Press, a suburban Chicago chain of newspapers, McWilliams had offered tapes of telephone conversations and pictures of various sites near Chicago, for a price. He had told the newspaper that he was going to produce a body before the reward offer expired. But he did not.

James Leaton said that the Morris Ferguson story, "just never panned out."

The reward was extended until September 25, 1981.

12

Charles Vorhees Tries Again

DURING the fourth year of her disappearance, Helen Brach's estate earned almost $4 million. The American Home Products stock paid dividends of $288,496. Seventeen Treasury bills and certificates came due or paid interest in 1980; those sums ranged from $30,000 to $200,000. One of the U.S. Bonds matured and paid half a million dollars. Everett Moore sold three of Mrs. Brach's elderly racehorses at auction that year. Misty JJ brought $3,000 at a sale in Ocala, Florida, and Vorhees Luv and Rhetts Bet went for $1,000 each in Mundelein, Illinois.

But, according to the statement Moore filed with the Circuit Court of Cook County, Helen Brach's expenditures exceeded her income. Moore spent $3,922,628.92, $35,821.39 more than the estate earned to maintain the Brach houses and reinvest money in certificates of deposit and Treasury bonds. About $100,000 went to care for her horses, though none of them won any money, and another $100,000 was paid to the Helen Brach Foundation, which in turn made gifts to animal welfare organizations. Federal income tax amounted to $54,500, and

Illinois state income tax was $6,803, in addition to the regular Social Security payments Moore made on behalf of Helen Brach. Approximately $16,000 went to Charles Vorhees to cover legal fees connected to his sister's disappearance.

News of Everett Moore's annual financial statement reached the newspapers just about the same time—a few days after the fourth anniversary, in 1981, of Helen Brach's disappearance—that it was learned that James Leaton, on behalf of Charles Vorhees, had petitioned Judge Budzinski's court to reinstate the $250,000 reward for two more years. Vorhees also wanted a $500,000 trust fund set up for himself out of his sister's assets. Charles Vorhees claimed that the trust would be "in consideration and in continuance of his sister's habits and desires and past favors and affections." To support that argument Leaton listed all of the gifts that Helen Brach had given her brother in the past. Vorhees said she had given him about $8,000 in jewelry and cash, the $55,000 home in Hopedale, ten cars worth $50,000, payment for his personal medical bills, vacation trips to Las Vegas and Florida and several ten-day to three-week cruises on a yacht complete with a private crew, and money for tuition at Kent State University for his two sons.

Five years after Helen Brach's disappearance, at a hearing held on February 23, 1982, Charles Vorhees's attorney, James Leaton petitioned Judge Budzinski, telling him that the cost of the new reward was not very significant considering that the bulk of the estate was "going to the dogs." Leaton reiterated his charge of a year ago that Richard Bailey had gone to South America to buy a horse and never brought one back. Mrs. Brach might have been murdered, he told the judge, when she threatened to expose the shady dealings of the horseman.

Defending Charles Vorhees's right to the half-million-dollar trust fund, Leaton explained that Mrs. Brach's brother's only source of income was his railroad pension and most of that money was used to pay for his sons' education. When Judge

Budzinski expressed disappointment that Vorhees was not in Chicago to make his appeal personally, Leaton said that his client was "too proud" to allow someone to pay for his trip from Hopedale and could not afford to come on his own.

The judge decided that it would be a waste of time to reestablish the reward offer and turned down Mr. Vorhees's request for a trust fund. He did allow $10,000 a year to be paid to the brother, however, in $2,500 installments.

Ironically, Charles Vorhees—who, in 1982, appeared to be desperately seeking some answers as to what may have happened to his sister—was the same person, who, with Jack Matlick, may have been destroying vital evidence when he burned her diaries and automatic writings back in March 1977. Helen Brach's own brother may have eliminated the only hope of convicting her killer when he set fire to that material.

Mr. Vorhees will presumably continue to enjoy his retirement in Ohio. As a rule he absolutely refuses to discuss his sister. When recently asked for an interview on the subject of Helen Brach, Vorhees screamed, "I don't know what you're talking about and I don't think she would either," before he hung up on the reporter.

13

The Horse Traders and Silas Jayne

THE horse traders were attractive suspects. The racetrack crowd had long been linked in the minds of the general public to organized crime. Chicago-area citizens had always imagined shadowy mobsters drugging animals, fixing races, and burning each other's stables. And if the whispered fables about Mafioso were not enough to convince people that the horse dealers were bad guys, then the stories about the Jayne gang were.

Everyone knew about the Jaynes. And the Bailey brothers associated with the Jaynes. The known association, combined with Richard Bailey's refusal to talk, led some people to believe that the horse traders had had something to do with Mrs. Brach's demise.

One reason the theory worked so well was motive. If one was a horse trader, it was thought, one did not need much of a motive to do something illegal. Just consider the story of Silas and his brother George, fifteen years younger. They were famous years before Helen Brach disappeared and Richard Bailey was questioned about her disappearance.

Silas and George Jayne, along with another brother, Frank, were called the "Jayne gang" by the residents of Woodstock, Illinois. During the 1930s and '40s they picked up railroad cars full of wild horses shipped from the West and drove the animals, cowboy style, through the town's streets to their ranch. There the worthy specimens were separated from the less fortunate beasts. The good horses were trained for riding, and the others were sent to a dogfood factory in Rockford. The Jaynes and their employees were known then for minor infractions: drinking and fighting.

Eventually the Jayne organization expanded to include the stabling and breeding of show horses. Trouble between George and Silas began brewing about 1959, when the two competed in horse shows. The prize money at these events did not amount to much—$1,000 for some events—but winning was potentially worth much more because it could increase the value of an animal by as much as $10,000. Friends, family, and business associates witnessed a number of arguments between the brothers during the 1960s. Finally, in 1967, one of the Jaynes' three sisters had a big family gathering, where Silas and George supposedly reconciled their differences after a long discussion in which Silas told George to quit drugging his horses because he was going to give the family business a bad name. The reconciliation was fragile, however, and within a few years Silas was reportedly going around trying to hire people to kill George. He told one potential assassin that he was mad at George because he would not repay the $25,000 he had loaned him to start his stable business.

In June 1965, someone planted a bomb in George Jayne's parked car near his Tri-Color Stables, in the Chicago suburb of Palatine, which exploded when Cherie Rude, a young model who rode one of George Jayne's show horses, started the engine. George accused Silas of accidentally killing the girl in an attempt to get him, but Silas was never linked to the woman's death.

Silas Jayne was arrested in connection with another plot, which police said was hatched just a few days after the car bombing. A horse trader from California, Stephen Grod, told sheriff's police that Silas had tried to hire him to kill George for $15,000. As a result, Silas was charged with conspiracy to commit a crime, but when the matter came to trial in spring 1966, Grod had unaccountably lost his memory and said that the $1,000 payment was money down on a horse and that the police had concocted the whole story about Silas.

Three and a half years later, in January 1969, Silas Jayne summoned the police to his home near Elgin, where they found a bullet-ridden corpse. George Jayne's phone number was written on a piece of paper in the dead man's pocket. Silas told the authorities that he killed Frank Mitchelle, a twenty-eight-year-old former bodyguard to George, in self-defense. Silas Jayne was not charged. Next, Silas hired three men—one of them had been a partner in a stable near Frankfort—and told them to kill George. That plot fell apart in August 1969.

Silas finally pressured Edward Nefeld, a former chief of detectives in south surburban Markham, Illinois, who owed Silas money for setting him up in a horse stable and auto repair and salvage business. In November Nefeld contacted Melvin Adams, a dishwasher from south suburban Posen, Illinois, and asked him if he would kill someone for money. When Adams agreed, Nefeld arranged a meeting for the next night with Joseph LaPlaca, an Elgin man who had worked as a handyman for Silas Jayne. Nefeld offered Adams $10,000 to kill George Jayne. In January 1970, Melvin Adams met Silas Jayne, who supposedly told him that he would have more work for him if he did a good job on George; Silas wanted to take care of two others who had testified against him on an indictment. He added that if, when he murdered George, George's wife or kids saw too much, he was to kill them, too. Melvin Adams went into training, following George Jayne around and shooting the pistols that Silas Jayne gave him at target practice.

Melvin Adams tried to back out of the deal, he said, but that caused the price to go up to $20,000. When Adams said he needed another man, Silas Jayne agreed and raised the price again to $30,000. Nefeld recruited Julius Barnes, a black Chicago laborer whom he had met when he arrested him several times in Markham. Barnes had always been released without being charged.

A plan to put a bomb in George Jayne's car was scrapped when it was decided that George would be a sitting duck for a sniper who targeted him at his home in Inverness. The traffic was light near the home and there were no streetlights. Adams and Barnes took target practice together. In September 1970, the pair went to George's home, but Barnes lost his gun on George's lawn. When Barnes and Adams returned to the house on October 28, Adams stayed in the car, about 100 feet away, while Barnes approached the home.

More than three years later, as part of an emotional courtroom drama, George Jayne's daughter Linda, then twenty-five years old, told what happened after that:

> "It was my brother George's sixteenth birthday. We arrived at the house at 5:45 P.M. My father and mother were there too. We talked for a while and then sat down for dinner at 6:15. After that we went into the living room and opened my brother's birthday gifts. We must have been there for another half-hour. After that I helped my mother clear the dishes from the living room. My father, my brother, and my husband went down into the basement to play pool. My mother stayed in the kitchen to finish up the dishes, and I went to the basement to join them. When I got there my father was sitting in a corner, working at his desk. My brother and my husband were playing pool. I made some Cokes and we set up the table to play bridge. At approximately 8:15 we sat down to play cards. By this time, my mother was with us. My brother had gone upstairs to do his homework. . . . We never did play cards. We dealt a few practice hands and then my father started shuffling the cards. . . . There was an explosion. My father stood up slowly. His eyes were open very wide. Then he sank slowly to the floor. There was blood spurting from his chest. I remember my mother screaming

his name and rushing to him. I ran to the phone to call a doctor. My husband ran to get towels to stop the blood. . . . [The explosion had come] through the basement window. . . . I had called for an ambulance. I went to my car and drove a few blocks away, so I could lead the ambulance directly to the house. They came within a few minutes. The next time I saw my father he was being carried out of the house on a stretcher. There was a sheet over his head. We followed the ambulance to Northwest Community Hospital, where he was pronounced dead. We were there about a half hour. Then we drove my mother back to the house.

The police suspected Silas Jayne immediately, but it was nearly a year before they got anywhere on the case. The Illinois Bureau of Investigation came up with Melvin Adams's license plate number and, eventually, with Adams. The dishwasher decided to cooperate rather than risk prosecution on a murder charge, was placed under heavy guard, and started making appearances before the Cook County Grand Jury. At the end of May 1971, Silas Jayne, Joseph LaPlaca, Edward Nefeld, and Julius Barnes were arrested. Silas Jayne was sixty-three years old then. Three days later Julius Barnes confessed that he had pulled the trigger. Nefeld pleaded guilty to conspiracy and was sentenced to three to ten years. LaPlaca, Jayne, and Barnes all pleaded not guilty and continued to be held without bond at Cook County Jail in Chicago for the next two years. Silas Jayne hired F. Lee Bailey to represent him when he finally went to trial the first week in May 1973.

For three weeks, F. Lee Bailey played to a courtroom packed with reporters, attorneys, and others who were curious to see in action the man who had defended such notables as Sam Sheppard, the "Boston Strangler," and Captain Ernest Medina. Melvin Adams, the star witness for the prosecution, spent hours and days on the stand telling his story. Silas Jayne was portrayed by Adams as a ruthless character who would go to any length to get rid of his brother. Once, Adams said, Jayne suggested mowing George down with a machine gun on an expressway. When Adams balked at the idea, Jayne told him, "If you get him alive, put him in a trunk and bring him to my house, and I'll bury him on my farm." Adams detailed how he and Barnes had gone to George Jayne's house and found it was too light outside on that evening of October 28, 1970. The two went to a restaurant where they had coffee and donuts and then returned to the house, where Adams watched Barnes go to the basement window and fire the gun. Then Adams contacted LaPlaca, who paid him $30,000 in two $15,000 installments. He gave $12,500 of that to Barnes.

The rest of the trial consisted mostly of witnesses substantiating Adams's story or repudiating it. Both Frank Jayne, Jr., and Frank Jayne, Sr., who was four years younger than his brother Silas, testified on Silas's behalf.

At the end of the proceedings Silas Jayne himself calmly took the stand. Silas Jayne—a stocky man with a rolling gait and a now-famous cryptic tongue—explained his differences with George and tried to persuade the jury that their problems had been solved in a friendly way. Originally they had gotten into a feud over George's sale of drugged horses, Silas said. But they had just called each other a lot of names. Even that animosity had ended, he continued, when they had a peace meeting at their sister's house in 1967.

It took the jury almost ten hours to decide that Silas Jayne was guilty of conspiracy to commit murder. LaPlaca was also found guilty of conspiracy. Barnes was found guilty of murder. If one considered the fact that Silas Jayne could have faced a murder rap and that he had already served twenty-three months and a week, the verdict was not the worst possible news. When a reporter asked attorney Bailey how it felt to lose one, he answered, "Lose one? You're forgetting what the jury did. Murder is a very serious charge. Conspiracy is a relatively minor felony. I would call that an acquittal."

Silas Jayne was sixty-six years old when he was sentenced to six to twenty years in jail. He would be eligible for parole in two years and three months.

Just prior to sentencing, F. Lee Bailey had asked the judge

not to "bury" Silas Jayne. The judge gave Jayne the maximum penalty, and he was sent to the Illinois facility at Menard.

The Jayne family disappeared from the news until the summer of 1976, when Light the Way, a six-year-old chestnut gelding, one of fifty show horses owned by Frank Jayne, Jr., was found poisoned at the Jayne's Northwestern Stables in Morton Grove. Light the Way had won two competitions at recent horse shows in Barrington Hills. At the time of the autopsy the horse trainer said that the poison could have been a pesticide, a medicine, or a substance devised specifically to kill the horse.

At the end of November that year, Marion Jayne sued her former brother-in-law for damages totaling $7.5 million. The bench trial lasted only ten minutes, and Judge Walter Kowalski ordered Silas, who was estimated to be worth about $2 million, to pay Mrs. Jayne $1 million. The widow told the judge that she and her children needed the money because they had had "financial difficulties" since George's death.

In the spring of 1978, Silas Jayne was brought back to Chicago to court to answer charges that he had hidden enough assets to pay the $1 million he owed Marion Jayne. Silas Jayne had no lawyer with him and asked for a six-month continuance. Instead, the judge gave him two days, saying that if he did not have an attorney by then, the court would appoint one. Marion Jayne's lawyer asked that Frank Jayne, Jr., be ordered to produce some personal and business records to uncover the assets of Silas Jayne.

After the hearing Silas Jayne went into the judge's chambers and in a closed session told him that two men were trying to kill him in jail. Then Silas held a fifteen-minute press conference in the corridor on the way out and said he was being discriminated against by Governor Thompson and should be released.

Two days later Silas went back to court, literally kicking and screaming. He had planned on holding another impromptu press conference in the Daley Center outside the courtroom. But the deputies pushed him through the hall and insisted he be handcuffed. Edward Kacmarek, chief of bailiffs, said that Silas Jayne had not been handcuffed on the trip from the downstate prison. "I chewed them out for that. I told a deputy to put handcuffs on him like any other prisoner here. When I said that, he threatened us. He said he'd beat the hell out of us. But I told him that in this building he belongs to me."

Bailiffs had hustled Jayne into a conference room on the twenty-fifth floor of the building, and reporters heard him shouting through the closed door, "If I have to fight, I have to fight. You're pushing me around."

Kacmarek was heard to say, "You threatened my life, buddy."

Judge Walter Kowalski, presiding over the discovery of Jayne's assets, commented, "Silas Jayne is a prisoner and not a celebrity." During his court appearance Jayne explained that he did not have any money. He had a small commissary account at the prison and a five-and-a-half-carat diamond ring that he was wearing. "F. Lee Bailey got a quarter of a million dollars," he said. "That was just a sample." Jayne sold his Northwestern Stables in Morton Grove to Frank Jayne, Jr., for $250,000. He said that he sold a stable in Norridge, Illinois, to his brother George in the 1960s for $90,000 and stables in Park Ridge to General Motors Corporation for $300,000. Jayne said his brother, Frank, Sr., had gotten a court order to seize a stable he owned near Elgin while he was in Cook County Jail awaiting trial and was unable to repay a $180,000 loan from his brother.

On February 15, it came to light that Silas Jayne was under investigation by a Milwaukee Grand Jury for being involved in setting two fires at the Nimrod Farms stable complex in Oconomowoc, Wisconsin. The first fire was set on April 11, 1976, killing thirty horses and causing $300,000 damage. Homer Adcock, the owner of Nimrod Farms, had moved the rest of the horses to a temporary barn, and that barn had burned on July 18, 1976. The Milwaukee authorities were looking into the possibility that a former cellmate of Jayne's, a forty-two-year-old burglar and arsonist, may have been paid $5,000 to set the fires and start a fight between Adcock and two Chicago-area brothers who breed horses. The police suspected that Jayne was feuding with the brothers but had been friendly with Adcock. Adcock said, "I have known the man [Jayne] for twenty-two years. I've hunted with him, fished with him, and shown horses with and against him in competition. He was supposed to be my friend." Adcock said that he thought the fires were started to "make me think the fire was the work of someone else and that I would retaliate against them and do someone else's dirty work. I have my suspicions, but there is no solid proof against anyone."

The parole board denied Silas Jayne immediate release but set a conditional release date of May 24, 1979, provided he continued with his good behavior.

Meanwhile, in May 1978 Silas Jayne went before the Grand Jury in Milwaukee and invoked the Fifth Amendment privilege to all its questions. That had been expected, but it was not expected that the jury would decide that the state didn't have a case. The U.S. attorney's office in Milwaukee said that the statements of Charles Johnson and Nick Guido, both convicted felons, were inconsistent regarding Silas Jayne. Basically, the story the criminals were telling was that Jayne had met with Guido and Johnson at the state correctional center in Vienna, Illinois. The main inconsistency in their story was that the two disagreed on the sum that Jayne promised for the arson contract. Guido said that it was $10,000; Johnson said it was $30,000. But the U.S. attorney's office investigators said that Guido was not present for part of the discussion because he had been sent by Jayne to escort Johnson's girlfriend to the vending machines. But Johnson's physical description of the scene of the Nimrod Farms arson was pretty accurate according to the police, and they were angry that the Grand Jury had elected not to prosecute Silas Jayne.

Jayne's lawyer commented, "When someone is serving a 60-

to 100-year sentence for a serious crime, one is likely to say anything to improve his prospective position before the parole board."

Later the Wisconsin authorities reconsidered the matter, and Silas Jayne was eventually indicted.

On May 24, 1979, at 5:00 A.M., his wife Dorothy and brother Frank drove to the Sheridan Correctional Center to pick up Silas Jayne. He had served eight years and two days. The warden, Neal MacDonald, walked him through the gate.

In April 1980 a trial was held in Benton, Illinois, and Silas Jayne was acquitted on two counts of conspiracy to commit arson and aiding and abetting arson.

14

Helen Brach and the Horse Traders

RICHARD Bailey did some business with the Jayne family, specifically with Frank Jayne, Jr., Silas's nephew, which connected Helen Brach directly or indirectly to the Jaynes. Perhaps, some of the officials close to the case surmised privately, Helen Brach found out that she was being gypped by the horse sellers or, worse, that they were cruel to animals. Perhaps, the theorists said, Helen Brach had told them that she intended to take them to court, and—because they knew she was wealthy enough to make their lives very difficult—they decided to remove her for good. Wittingly or unwittingly, the story went, Matlick could have been brought into the deal to set her up. One version said that Jack Matlick picked her up at the Kahler Hotel in Rochester, Minnesota, and delivered her to her horsemen associates at some remote spot they had agreed upon. This suggestion meant that someone else must have used her Northwest Airlines plane ticket to O'Hare Airport. According to that reasoning, Helen Brach was somewhere between Glenview and Rochester, Minnesota. After she was taken care of, the story continued, Matlick was left to fend for himself, which was one way of accounting for his careless explanation of what happened over the weekend of February 18, 1977.

Coincidentally, Frank Jayne III, age twenty-two, came to a mysterious end during the summer of 1980. He was on his way to the Kentucky Derby with two women friends and was last seen alive on May 3. His body was fished from a pit near Interstate 65 on June 24. Young Jayne's father, Frank, Jr., reported him missing to the Morton Grove police five weeks after he disappeared. The report said only that he was "lost somewhere in Indiana," but that information never made it to the National Crime Information Computer.

The young man's two companions said that he had become ill about 1:30 A.M. on Derby Day. They had stopped the auto, and he had walked away from the car. When he did not come back, the women continued south on the interstate, stopped at a rest area near the Boone-Clinton county line and called the sheriff. The sheriff's deputies said that the search took a long time because the women could not remember where Jayne had gotten out of the car.

About a week before the drowning was reported, Frank Jayne, Jr.'s ranch house in Wayne, Indiana, had been destroyed by a fire police suspected was an arson.

No one was ever charged or prosecuted for involvement in the death or the fire.

Glenview's Sergeant Joseph Baumann, the ranking authority in the Helen Brach case since the retirement of Police Chief Bartlett in 1980, did not say that he subscribed to any theory about Mrs. Brach's disappearance, but he seemed to have gone along with the idea that the horse traders had done it. "Mr. Bailey has not answered any questions for us ever," Baumann said. "The only people that would know about Mrs. Brach probably fear for their lives. [The fact that no one has come up with information and claimed the reward money] leads you to believe money was not the motive. The only thing I can say, if Mrs. Brach is dead, the only motive I can think of was that she was the type of person who would go to the authorities.

"Some people here in Chicago and Fort Lauderdale indicated that she would call them every day. Knowing this, I find it is difficult for me to say that Mrs. Brach came back to the Village of Glenview. She was asking the clerk in the boutique [in Rochester] to rush because her houseman was waiting outside. Mr. Matlick denied that he was ever in Rochester and there is nothing to prove that he was." On his desk in his office at the police headquarters, Baumann had a pile of photographs of spray-painted messages that accused Richard Bailey of the murder. There were no new messages after the summer of 1979, when John Menk tried to take a deposition from Bailey.

If one stretched his imagination, he might be able to tie Morris Ferguson to Silas Jayne. Conceivably the two could have crossed paths during the time they spent in various Illinois jails. This was the reason the Ferguson tale seemed so appealing to those who felt that Mrs. Brach's death was linked to the horse traders.

Menk, the author of the original hypothesis, has always stood by his idea about Bailey and his cohorts. Menk most recently has said that the chief problem in the case was "the inability of anyone to articulate a definite motive. The principal suspects turned out to be the people who had the most to gain by keeping her alive. It has gotten down to a cerebral problem. The familiar landmarks are not there.

"The two principal suspects—both close to her before her death—both declined to testify in a civil proceeding on the grounds it might incriminate. To take the Fifth Amendment—[and I'm not] attempting to impugn or criticize—it's only human to say it stimulates our curiosity. When I examined Mr. Matlick under oath he declined to respond to any question about whether he made reservations on the flight to Florida, whether he generally worked Saturday and Sunday, why he was at the house on Saturday and Sunday, did he prepare a group of checks for her to sign a few days before she disappeared.

"Bailey wouldn't even give his name.

"I'm quite sure it was a conspiracy. She was a circumspect

lady and very distrusting of strangers, based upon my conversation with her friends. She was not inclined to do anything out of the ordinary. It would be too much for one person to do all this; it's much more likely that someone she trusted inveigled her into a situation from which she could not extricate herself.

"By all accounts, Helen Brach was a relatively normal, late-middle-aged woman who had a great deal of money she was trying to do some good with. . . .

"The horse crowd can be ruthless and cruel."

In order to accept the idea that the horse traders did it, one had to accept a couple of other notions too. First, one had to believe that Helen Brach was able to cause these men to become irate enough with her to want to murder her. For the horse traders, as John Menk pointed out, Helen Brach was the goose laying the golden eggs. There was no evidence that she had any intention of ceasing her purchase of horses, worthless or otherwise. While there was not even the flimsiest motive for them to want to kill her, the horse traders had one big reason—her bottomless bank account—to make them want to keep her alive.

Also, all of the rumors about the horse traders doing in Mrs. Brach seemed to have stemmed from the horse traders themselves. Either they were attempting to incriminate one another or they simply liked their image as tough, ruthless killers enough that they decided that taking credit for Helen Brach's demise would be safe and would enhance their reputations.

Many of the stories about the horse traders and Mrs. Brach have been traced back to comments they have made themselves around various suburban stables or in late-night conversation at the Blue Moon Ballroom and Lounge in Elgin, where Silas Jayne and his friends in the polo set went to socialize.

At least one member of that set has shown himself capable of murder. But if the horsemen claim they played a part in this mystery, that is yet to be established. The same can be said about their innocence.

15

Jack Matlick and the Perfect Crime

JACK Matlick was always the primary suspect in the early years of the investigation. After a while he was written off because he was just a small-time guy, possibly capable of conspiracy or a mistake but not of murder. Some of those who have met Matlick have described him as cooperative and perhaps a bit frightened of something or someone.

But Jack Matlick knew more than he said he knew. In the beginning he was very talkative about the weekend with Mrs. Brach before she disappeared. Glenview Police Sergeant Baumann smiled when he insisted that Matlick had always been very cooperative with the authorities. And Matlick apparently talked openly at first with Ernie Rizzo, the private detective, and with Mrs. Brach's brother, Charles Vorhees. Very few things in his story make sense, however, and parts of it are simply dumbfounding.

Everything Jack Matlick said that Helen Brach did after she left Rochester was totally inconsistent with her normal behavior. And everything he said he did was inconsistent with his normal behavior around Mrs. Brach. If Helen Brach did not make or receive a phone call over the weekend of February 18–21, 1977, she was not near a telephone and she was not at the Glenview residence. For Jack Matlick to stay in the house with Mrs. Brach there was most irregular—more evidence that she was not there that weekend. There was no "mystery man" who appeared that Sunday night; Richard Bailey seemed to have been in Florida. It was preposterous to think that Helen Brach went to the airport on Monday morning without letting anyone know she was coming, without any luggage, and without an airline reservation. And she never wrote those checks; the amounts and their purposes were ridiculous. She was conservative, and she was tight with her money, at least when it came to spending it on human beings. The checks were obviously forged. But, instead of saying that he found the checks on a table or that Mrs. Brach had left them for him, Matlick said he watched her sign them.

Matlick had been living with Helen Brach for twenty years; he must have known her habits. Why was his story so odd?

Not only was Jack Matlick's version of what happened peculiar in ways that tended to impeach him; it was also just *plain* peculiar. For instance, he volunteered the fact that he had put some jewelry in a safe deposit box on Monday, after Mrs. Brach supposedly left for Florida. He had access to a hoard of valuables that could be sold and never traced, but as far as anyone knew, the jewelry was all there when the court opened the box three months later.

The houseman's behavior after February 18, 1977, was so erratic that it gave rise to plenty of farfetched ideas about what may have happened. There were about twenty-three phone calls from the Glenview estate in the two weeks around that period. Even though Helen Brach had gone to Florida for an extended stay, Matlick hired a full-time cook after she left. Ernie Rizzo thought that the cook might actually *be* Helen Brach—that she had, for some reasons of her own, decided to go incognito. Surmising that she might have been able to change her appearance but not her body, the private detective made a chalk mark representing Mrs. Brach's height on the back doorway of the Glenview house and waited, hidden close by, until the cook went through the door in order to see how she stood. The cook was much shorter than Mrs. Brach.

Ernie Rizzo's final conclusion was that Mrs. Brach had become a missing person at the hands of Jack Matlick. "It was a personality thing," he shrugged. "She was moving to Florida and she didn't need Matlick anymore. He had twenty years on the job."

Another observer, a one-time neighbor of Helen Brach's, said that Matlick was in and out of the Glenview house at all times of the day and night. She called it "a lover's quarrel." Matlick, she supposed, killed Helen Brach in a fit of rage and than managed to dispose of the body.

There were titillating bits of evidence to support this theory, but none of them went anywhere: for example, the whole notion that Matlick purchased the meat grinder attachment for the blender, processed Helen Brach's body, and fed her to her dogs. But the meat grinder attachment was too small, the task would have been impossible, and the police checked the instrument in a laboratory and found nothing.

Matlick had shampooed the car interior, but again the police found nothing.

The decorators had come to redo part of the house and replace a rug, but there had been nothing unusual about the job.

Of course, the biggest obstacle to proving that Jack Matlick did it is that there was no body. For fifty-seven days prior to the disappearance the temperature had not gone above five degrees. The ground was actually three feet of ice. Ernie Rizzo started looking in cemeteries for freshly dug graves. He said that was the best place in the world to hide a body. But he did not have any luck. Rizzo still thought she was somewhere around Glenview, though. "There are hundreds of bodies lying around," he said. "There's a list this long of what they've pulled out of the Skokie Lagoon alone. In twenty-five years they'll come across her body."

"At one point Matlick was a real blabbermouth," Rizzo said.

In his opinion, had Matlick been treated as a suspect from the start, there may have been a chance for a solution. But instead the handyman was allowed to stay in the house, with whatever evidence was there. After the police told Matlick that he was a suspect and needed a lawyer, Matlick got a lawyer. The lawyer told him to shut up.

If Jack Matlick murdered Helen Brach, he may, in his clumsy way, have committed the perfect crime.

16

The End of the Cold Trail

IF you try to look at the Helen Vorhees Brach case from the standpoint of a criminal investigator, there are some terrible obstacles that have to be overcome to bring the case to a legal resolution. First of all, as the Glenview police have always taken great care to point out, the investigation into the disappearance of Helen Brach was a missing-person inquiry. From the outset, from the time the trail was still warm, authorities' hands were tied. At times Baumann and Bartlett and the rest of the Glenview police investigators were made to look silly by some outsiders—particularly Ernie Rizzo—because there was so little they could do. Much of the information they had gotten turned out to be from people who might have been suspects. Private investigators and the press may have come up with more information than anyone on the side of law enforcement, but most of that information would be totally useless in court anyway.

"The chain of evidence was totally destroyed," Ernie Rizzo said. Jack Matlick had ample opportunity to take evidence out of the house and put evidence back into the house. Nobody seemed to know—or nobody seemed to want to talk about—the contents or the amount of material that Charles Vorhees and Jack Matlick burned in the furnace.

An army of the curious, including the security people who have access to the Glenview estate right now, have been through the house. Helen Brach's will made the rounds of police, lawyers, and reporters before it became a public document. If Mrs. Brach's body was found lying on her kitchen floor tomorrow, it seems highly unlikely that there would be a criminal prosecution as a result. The body would be just one more piece of physical evidence that could not be linked to any living person. You have to remember that the disappearance of Helen Brach has been studied carefully by a host of publicity-conscious lawyers and politicians. They do not take cases to court unless they think that they are going to come away from a trial looking better than they did going in.

The suggestion surfaces time and again that the present Cook County state's attorney, Richard Daley, should convene a grand jury and offer Jack Matlick immunity. If Matlick is part of the conspiracy, it is thought, he will name the perpetrators of the foul deed. But what if he *is* the perpetrator of the foul deed? The principle behind the immunity idea is that half a loaf is better than none. But in a case like this that tenet simply does not apply to a political institution like the state's attorney's office. As one prominent Chicago attorney, who is a former prosecutor and a former judge in Cook County Circuit Court, has said, "I'd sure hate to be the prosecutor who brought some guy in and gave him immunity and then the guy confessed to murder." He is absolutely right. There is always the possibility that you could still bring that person to trial on some other charge like perjury, but there is no politician who is feebleminded enough to believe that that kind of incident would not prove to be very embarrassing in front of the voting public. A half a loaf, then, could make a prosecutor look very dumb. Former Cook County State's Attorney Bernard Carey refused to try it. And Sergeant Joe Baumann has not had much encouragement from Richard Daley's office.

The Morris Ferguson fiasco makes it even less likely that the state's attorney's office would want to get involved with the Glenview police at this point. Baumann did not come out of that situation looking like the most reliable source of information. Poor Helen Brach. Leads like the Morris Ferguson story only add insult to injury.

But Baumann continues his investigation, hoping to solve the crime—if there was a crime, he says—before he retires and waiting for the prosecutors to give him a call.

Everett Moore continues to manage the estate and all its properties except the Continental Bank Trust. If Mrs. Brach were to return tomorrow, she could continue her lifestyle as it was in 1977, without having to right matters first.

Belton Mouras continues his work on behalf of animals, with generous annual contributions from the Helen Brach Foundation. If the situation remains the same until 1984, the Animal Protective Institute may end up a very well-endowed organization.

Ernie Rizzo's private detective business is doing very well. Rizzo is often seen on Chicago television programs. In fact, he went on one show a couple of years ago and predicted correctly that Kristin had shot J. R. Ewing, on TV's *Dallas*. Rizzo has become an expert at finding snatched children in child custody cases.

Continental Bank has diversified the Helen Vorhees Brach Trust portfolio, and the income from that money has increased.

Arthur Gorov considers the mystery a dead issue. He has an opinion about who did it, but he will not state it. If Gorov ever gets any good leads on the case, he said, he is committed to calling his daughter, who is a journalist, before he does anything else.

John Menk, who moved out of the Sears Tower to another Loop office in the summer of 1981, still ruminates often about the Helen Brach case. He admits that he is an amateur sleuth, has stated his theory about what happened to Helen Brach, and is bothered that a murder may go unpunished.

Silas Jayne wants to get back into the stable business, but, because of his reputation, he is having some trouble. He told an interviewer a couple of years ago, ". . . Now my nephew, Silas III, is in the business, and, see, I'd like to steer that Grand Champion Stables his way. That's why I want that stable, for the name, for the younger generation. I don't need no more money. I'm seventy-three years old. I don't need no more prestige."

Jack Matlick is living in a community near Pittsburgh, Pennsylvania, reportedly by himself. The suburb, which is ironically only a couple of hours' drive from Helen Brach's hometown of Hopedale, bears a distinct resemblance to Schaumburg, the northwest suburb of Chicago where Matlick lived for so many years. It is an old farm area, with a quaint little town set in the middle of a large rural space, and new developments are popping up where some of the farmland used to be. Jack Matlick lives in one of the new sections. Baumann says that the Glenview police know exactly how to get in touch with him in Pennsylvania.

For a small group of people, the disappearance of Helen Brach has become a kind of game, a puzzle to be solved over and over again in many different ways. But that was always the tragedy of the situation. Nobody really cared about *her*. If someone had really cared, if someone had missed her immediately after she vanished, there might have been a chance of getting to the bottom of this mystery.

Perhaps Helen Brach understood the way things were better than anyone could have guessed and for that reason left her fortune to needy animals.

Luvey Brach, a very friendly, medium-sized white sheep dog, used to miss Helen Brach a lot. In 1977 Luvey was turned over to the Animal Protective Institute. For a time, she lived in a kind of halfway house for animals in Berwyn, Illinois. Then she was boarded at the In-Town Pet Motel, a deluxe animal shelter in nearby Oak Park, Illinois. But she moped around there, and eventually it was decided that the best thing for Luvey would be a good home.

In August 1978, when Luvey was five years old, she was named "Pet of the Week" by an Oak Park newspaper. Ramona Fox, Larry Fox's wife and Laura and Lacey Fox's mother, thought that it was about time the family had a dog. So Larry and Ramona went to see about Luvey. They did not know Luvey's surname at first, but, as Ramona said, "We knew right away that she wasn't an ordinary dog."

The Foxes were interviewed at length, and the man from the animal shelter explained to them that, if they incurred any major medical expense with Luvey or if she had any medical problems, Helen Brach's estate would take care of the bills. The Foxes were told that, should Helen Brach reappear, they would have to give up the dog.

Luvey has been her buoyant self almost since the day she moved in with the Fox family. The depressed, nervous habits she had went away during the first few weeks. The family still has the pink rhinestone collar with the dog bone shaped charm that says, "Luvey Brach. Call Collect." But the new name tag that Luvey wears simply says, "Luvey."

Larry says, "Generic dogfood is quite a comedown from filet mignon, but we're a happy family."

17

A Final Resting Place

U NIONPORT'S main street runs along a narrow, winding incline. The houses lined up in a row are mostly made of wood and are almost all more than fifty years old. The trees that shade the lane are lush and green, and arch upward to form a tunnel over the pavement. You would imagine that this place looked the same a century ago and will probably stay this way for another hundred years, though the aluminum siding on some of the houses might be replaced by something better, and the styles of the automobiles parked in the gravel driveways alongside the houses will change or perhaps disappear altogether. The big trees give way at the end of the road as the street curves into a clearing. On one side a neat row of tract houses have been built. Across the way is the cemetery.

There are about fifty graves in the hillside. The Vorhees' friends and relatives have been buried here since the 1800s.

When her mother died in 1966, Helen Vorhees Brach went to work on a family monument.

It took four years to complete the spectacular granite and

marble tomb at a cost of about half a million dollars. The edifice sits at the very highest point on the hill. Behind it there is a steep drop down into a valley crowded with vegetation and clusters of trees. It is a gravesite with quite a view. Three arches, supported by a group of classic stone columns, stretch over the raised marble platform that contains six crypts.

Inscribed in the closest arch is VORHEES, in the next GOD IS LOVE, and in the third BRACH. Four messages are carved onto posts that border the tombs. The two nearest the Vorhees arch say: THROUGH THE ARCHWAY OF LIFE ETERNAL, MAY I BE NEARER MY GOD TO THEE, and DEATH IS THE ARCHWAY TO ETERNAL LIFE. SAVIOR LET ME WALK WITH THEE. Helen Brach's mother and father rest here. Each burial place is marked by a raised stone in the shape of a casket. At the top of Walter Samuel Vorhees's grave the triangular badge of a grange member is etched in the stone. It says that he was a member for sixty-three of his eighty-eight years. There are a bunch of lilies drawn beneath this picture and his name, the names of his parents, and his birth and death dates. The carving on Daisy Rowland Vorhees's tomb shows an angel bent over a clump of flowers and reads, AN ANGEL VISITED THE EARTH ONE DAY AND TOOK A BELOVED FLOWER AWAY.

The post at the far edge of the monument, next to the spot where Frank Brach is buried, says simply: MAY ETERNAL LIFE BE GRANTED THIS SERVANT WHO WAS ONE OF GOD'S GOOD SAMARITANS. Frank Brach's tombstone is decorated with a relief of a factory complex complete with smokestacks. In truth, it looks more like the Scio Pottery Factory than the plant on Kinzie Street, but the legend underneath says, BRACH'S CANDYLAND; CHICAGO, ILLINOIS. His birth and death dates are inscribed below the factory, followed by a testimonial that describes him as the LOVING HUSBAND OF HELEN VORHEES BRACH. A FOUNDER AND CHIEF EXECUTIVE DEVELOPING THE WORLD'S LARGEST CANDY FACTORY, E. J. BRACH & SONS, RECOGNIZED AS A LEADER IN THE CANDY INDUSTRY, A PIONEER IN AVIATION, A HUMANITARIAN AND A PHILANTHROPIST.

Helen Brach took great care when she made this monument. She traveled to Vermont to pick out the stone and hired the artist who would fashion it. But nowhere are the great pains she took more obvious than in the final resting place she prepared for herself. The expression carved to the right hand says, FATHER, I PRAY I MAY BE WORTHY TO BE NEAR MY LOVED ONES WHO ARE WITH THEE. Her gravesite looks like a great engraved gift of Valentine's Day candy, reminiscent of the opening credits on the old "I Love Lucy" show. A bower of roses is contained in the length of the rectangle. It is tied at the bottom with a sculpted ribbon and inside the bouquet the name HELEN MARIE VORHEES BRACH is written in lavish script, slanted up toward Frank Brach's grave.

At the foot of each Brach crypt there are two small square stone markers where Candy and Sugar, both beloved dogs of Helen Brach, are buried. Mrs. Brach lost Candy the same year she lost Frank.

The row of red plastic carnations that forms the front border of Helen Brach's gravesite are beginning to droop. (Helen loved artificial flowers and had them in all her homes.) The plastic flowers are keeping the advancing crabgrass and weed stalks at bay, at least for the time being.

The irony of this scene is that Helen Marie Vorhees Brach will probably never be buried here—in this place she had fixed so lovingly for herself, surrounded by her husband, her parents, and her pets.